Marilyn St.Clair

John Laskowski's Tales from the Hoosier Locker Room

John Laskowski
with
Stan Sutton

Sports Publishing L.L.C.
www.SportsPublishingLLC.com

Direction of production: Susan M. Moyer
Project manager: Greg Hickman
Developmental editor: Doug Hoepker
Copy editor: Cynthia L. McNew
Dust jacket design: Kenneth J. O'Brien

ISBN: 1-58261-584-5

Printed in the United States.

SPORTS PUBLISHING L.L.C.
www.SportsPublishingLLC.com

Acknowledgments

The history of Indiana University basketball has been documented for nearly a century by writers who followed the fortunes of the IU team, whether it be referred to as the Crimsons, the Hurryin' Hoosiers, or, more lately, just plain Hoosiers. By any name Indiana basketball has received national recognition, not only for its success on the court but because of the vast audience that follows its fortunes.

This book is an attempt to compile special memories of the men who called themselves Hoosiers, whether it was in the days of the underhand free throw or the skyhook. Former players contacted by the authors were gracious in their help, usually showing that while their bodies may age, their memories are largely unfrayed by time. Such is the case with William Silberstein, who played in the 1930s, as well as with such fellow Hoosiers as Bob Leonard, Joby Wright, Gary Long and Jimmy Rayl.

A special thanks goes to the IU Media Relations Office, director Jeff Fanter and basketball director Pete Rhoda for making their archives available. These include student managers' logbooks from the 1920s and newspaper clippings from those days through the Mike Davis era. A special thanks to former sports information director Tom Miller for his vast memories of IU basketball and to such storytellers as the original television "Voice of the Hoosiers," Paul Lennon.

Contents

Foreword

John Laskowski's Tales of the Hoosier Locker Room will appeal
to Indiana fans who have spent their lifetime as fans of the Hoosiers, but it also will appeal to those who have joined the band-
wagon more recently, as in the case of this middle-aged trans-
plant from Alabama. Laskowski and co-author Stan Sutton have
woven together articles of humor and nostalgia that will stir the
memories of all Hoosiers and remind them of the thrills provided by their favorite players and coaches.

These pages cover Indiana basketball from its earliest games
against Purdue to our 2002 march to the NCAA Tournament's
championship game. Laskowski's reminiscences from IU's greatest years blend with memories of the school's greatest games and
greatest players. Remembrances of Don Schlundt, Jimmy Rayl,
Steve Alford and Damon Bailey are mixed with offbeat stories
about IU's early days on television and the sacrifices made by
Indiana players during World War II. Hoosier lettermen recall
the funnier sides, and often caring sides, of Branch McCracken
and Bob Knight.

Some of the more memorable players, such as Dane Fife,
weren't necessarily Indiana's greatest, but their actions and antics
make for enjoyable reading.

Mike Davis
Head Basketball Coach
Indiana University

Chapter 1

How the Hoosiers Got that Way

Indiana has been a state of many divisions since it joined the union in 1816. U.S. Highway 40, which runs from Richmond on the east boundary to Terre Haute on the West, conveniently splitting Indianapolis through the middle, divides the state into North and South regions. While the split hardly reaches Mason-Dixon proportions, it allows Hoosiers to think of themselves as Northern Indiana residents or Southern ones.

An even bigger separation divides those who live in rural areas from Hoosiers who have settled into more metropolitan lifestyles. Except for those in The Region—a complex of Chicago suburbs including Hammond, East Chicago, Whiting, Gary and Portage—most Hoosiers think of themselves as rural. Even longtime Indianapolis residents, who recall when their hometown was unkindly called Naptown, have deep ties with agricultural Indiana.

Regardless of their home sites, Indiana residents pretty much see themselves as equal. Former Indiana football player Jay Davis, a native of Rushville, perhaps best described the feelings of many of these Hoosiers.

"I consider myself a city boy, but there's a farm right down the street," he said.

Since 1911, the year the Indiana high school basketball tournament was launched, basketball exceeded all other interests in Hoosierland. Barbershops were the sites of discussions about corn crops, the price of eggs and the pastor's sermon from the previous Sunday. But mostly they provided the setting for discussions, and arguments, about basketball.

Surely, bragging rights started in Indiana.

The Indiana high school tournament consisted of one class until 1998, and another dividing point existed: People either lived in cities where their favorite team had a chance to win a state championship, or they lived in a town where it was impossible. But even before tiny Milan won the 1954 title, every fan believed his or her team had a chance, although those in places such as Muncie and Kokomo knew it was realistic.

Interest in Indiana University basketball was an offspring of this lifestyle. The four weeks of the high school tournament were televised before IU games were shown on the tube. The NCAA Tournament was founded in 1939, three years after the Frankfort Hot Dogs established themselves as probably the best high school team in Indiana history.

By then another dividing line had formed between in-state residents, who had to decide whether they favored the Indiana Hoosiers or the Purdue Boilermakers. Feelings over this issue would grow until nearly no one was neutral about the rivalry. The West Lafayette university always had a strong fan base in northwestern Indiana and among the farming communities, a result of Purdue's agricultural and engineering schools.

IU fans were spread more evenly around the state, partly because the university produced doctors, lawyers, businessmen and teachers who would establish homes in various settings.

Bragging rights reached a new level.

Some houses were divided. One Bloomington couple endured a Saturday in March when their respective colleges, Indiana and Purdue, played each other on the same day their high schools, Franklin and Speedway, met in the state high school finals.

During the early days of the rivalry, the Boilermakers were so dominant that it now would take some 15 years without losing for the Hoosiers to assume the series lead.

Purdue launched its basketball program in 1896, while Indiana didn't fall in line until the turn of the century, when Purdue won nine straight games over the Hoosiers. By 1914, the Boilermakers had a 22-3 lead in the rivalry.

Indiana since has cut into the disadvantage and, in the estimation of the IU fans, overwhelmed any embarrassment by capturing five NCAA championships. Despite 21 Big Ten championships (Indiana has 20), the Boilermakers' only ventures into the Final Four were in 1969 and '80.

Indiana won its first national title in 1940 and followed with a second under coach Branch McCracken in 1953. By that time the then Hurryin' Hoosiers had slipped ahead of Purdue in the consciousness of many in-state fans, but by the early '70s Purdue again was laying claim to being *the* Indiana university.

Purdue opened Mackey Arena in 1967, eight years after Indiana had abandoned its fieldhouse on Seventh Street and moved into a new one off Fee Lane. However, Purdue had a 14,000-seat arena specifically for basketball while the Hoosiers still were playing in a multipurpose building that was intended to be stop-gap housing.

The Boilermakers enhanced their position in the rivalry by recruiting three successive Indiana Mr. Basketballs. Dennis Brady of Lafayette Jefferson, Billy Keller of Indianapolis Washington, and Rick Mount of Lebanon rejected the advances of McCracken and Lou Watson, a former assistant who replaced the Big Sheriff after the 1964-65 season.

McCracken had outstanding teams in the early '60s, but his 1963-64 club fell to 9-15. Watson's first team won only four of 14 Big Ten games but rebounded to win the Big Ten in 1966-67. That was followed by three straight losing campaigns in which the Hoosiers won only 26 games.

For a number of seasons Indiana had successfully recruited several members of each year's Indiana All-Star team. However, suddenly the Boilermakers were making inroads and getting the upper hand, especially with Mount, one of the nation's most exciting players.

Indiana faced one of the major challenges in its basketball history, which was complicated when Watson's back problems forced assistant Jerry Oliver to coach most of the 1969-70 season. Watson stepped down after the Hoosiers bounced back with a 17-7 record the next season, and an exhaustive search was carried out for a new man who could right a listing ship and counter the recent gains made by Purdue.

The Hoosiers found that man at the United States Military Academy at West Point, N.Y. Bob Knight would not only return Indiana to its past glories but exceed them in a 29-year career during which cream and crimson flowed down the face of college basketball.

Hoosiers Find a Disciplinarian

The months surrounding the hiring of a new basketball coach may have been the most crucial in IU history. Two years earlier the Indiana football program had been flourishing, when a boycott by the team's African-American players threw things into mayhem. Watson, only 46, was the focal point of some unrest on the Hoosier varsity. Some players complained about alleged favorable treatment toward superstar sophomore George McGinnis, who would turn professional after that season. Others were unhappy about a lack of playing time, hardly a new problem at any university.

Most of the IU student body had enrolled during the tumultuous days of the Vietnam War, an era when placards of all descriptions were hoisted around campus. Watson had far more friends than enemies. He had displayed a dogged determination as a player, and when he became a coach, most of his players were ready to go to war with him.

*Forward George McGinnis averaged 31 points a game during
his sophomore season and then promptly left for the Indiana Pacers.
Photo courtesy IU Archives*

Bob Leonard was an example, saying, "Here's a guy who had been in the second wave of the Normandy invasion. You think he wasn't tough?"

A coaching search, headed by athletics director Bill Orwig, was surrounded by heavy speculation. The Indiana job was one of the more prized in the nation and had known only two head coaches in the previous quarter-century.

As a later IU president, Dr. Myles Brand, would say 29 years later: "We don't name basketball coaches very often around here. When we do, we make sure that we've made the right choice."

From the start, the university appeared to have one criterion for Watson's successor. As sports editor Bob Hammel wrote in the *Bloomington Herald-Telephone*:

Perhaps the single, leading attribute being sought in Indiana University's basketball coaching hunt is a demonstrated ability to floor a disciplined team . . . That may not be exactly the sort of change players had in mind, but it's the inevitable result under present circumstances. The "tight ships" are the ones that are running best, even in these enlightening days.

Orwig was quoted as saying, "I am looking for a coach that teaches disciplined basketball. If a coach teaches discipline on the floor, then he teaches discipline off the floor."

Knight's Appointment Surprises Many

Bob Knight's name didn't surface in the early speculation. Oliver applied for the job, and former IU All-American Bob Leonard, then coach of the Indiana Pacers, turned it down. Former IU All-American Bill Garrett, who had coached Indianapolis Crispus Attucks to a state high school championship, was among the applicants, but North Carolina State coach Norm Sloan soon surfaced as the favorite—at least in the rumor mill.

Sloan was a product of Indianapolis Lawrence Central High who had been recruited to North Carolina State by former Indiana coach Everett Dean. Sloan had replaced Press Maravich there as the head coach in 1965, shortly before Press coached his famous son, Pete, at Louisiana State.

As the coaching search evolved, one report surfaced that Sloan and California coach Jim Padgett were the finalists. But it was Knight, whose reputation for discipline would only grow over the years, who turned out to be the man.

The former Ohio State reserve was 30 years old and had greatly enhanced his reputation since West Point named him the nation's youngest head coach at 24. During those six seasons the Cadets posted a 102-50 record, even while academy restrictions prevented anyone taller than six feet six from enrolling as a freshman.

Knight had played on one of college basketball's greatest teams. Led by Jerry Lucas, John Havlicek, Larry Siegfried and Mel Nowell, the Buckeyes were the 1960 NCAA champions and were upset in the title game by Cincinnati each of the next two years. Knight made no pretense of his value as a player, but his view from the bench enabled him to absorb great things.

"I was an average player. I wasn't quick and I didn't jump well, and I think I could be a candidate for [coach Fred] Taylor's all-time bad defensive team," Knight said upon his hiring.

Player was Warned in Advance

A veteran group of players awaited Knight's arrival, but the first one to have a clue as to what lay ahead was Joby Wright, a senior who had averaged 17.6 points as a junior under Watson. He had heard about the West Point coach while trying out for the Pre-Olympic Development Team at the Air Force Academy.

"One night during the course of team selection, somebody got some beer and whatever. Guys went out and we just raised all kinds of noise," Wright said. "The next day they brought every-

Joby Wright had heard tales of Bobby Knight the disciplinarian, but after meeting his new coach, Wright quickly saw the soft inner side of Knight. Photo courtesy of IU Archives

body together and really read the riot act. They said the next time that happened they were going to send everybody home. I think maybe somebody may have been sent home."

One of the coaches, John Bach of Pennsylvania, then told the players of a shuddering possibility.

"Bach had this gift of gab. After the incident Bach was talking to maybe 10 of us and he said, 'You guys think you're tough, but let me tell you something. If this one guy was here, this one coach—you don't even know who he is. His name is Bobby Knight. He's the coach at Army,'" Wright recalled.

"He started telling these stories about Knight and we were all laughing. He did this and he did that. Bach was telling the things that happened in camp when Knight caught a kid goofing off. He would make a kid do this or do that. Our attitude was, 'Yeah, right!'" Joby said.

Before Indiana hired its new coach, president John Ryan communicated frequently with Wright concerning the coaching situation.

"President Ryan had just gotten the job and he told me, 'We have a new coach, Bob Knight, from West Point,'" Joby recalled. "I said, 'Oh, man, I've heard of that guy.' The guys got together and they asked if I knew anything about him and I said, 'Yeah, I've heard about him and he's a pretty tough guy.'"

All of the Hoosiers were phoning various contacts to learn more about the youthful disciplinarian.

George McGinnis, the Hoosiers' brilliant forward, already had made his decision to turn professional, and Ed Daniels, like Wright a native of Savannah, Ga., had decided to transfer to Marquette.

"I think if you'd ask both of those guys about their decisions, there's no doubt they'd have regrets," Wright insisted.

A Special Time in History

Knight's arrival in Bloomington coincided with a period of turmoil across the country. A year earlier, four students had been killed by Ohio National Guardsmen during a demonstration at Kent State.

Around the Indiana campus, placards protested America's involvement in the Vietnam War. The Bloomington City Council became an extension of campus feelings as liberal representatives were elected, partly because of the student vote.

"It was '70-71. You had students taking over administration buildings," Wright said. "We didn't wear long pants or tattoos. We wore the big Afros and had the hippies. We had the Black Panthers. It was just a lot of different things going on in society. And here's the coach from West Point, and people didn't know where that was coming from."

Wright was the first player called in to meet the new coach.

"I went in and I had my Afro and my blue jeans. I was going to show this guy. He's never seen no tough guy like me. I'm going to test him," Wright vowed. "And the first time I met him he read me the riot act. Coach went off—'You're going to go to class! You have to toe the line!'—Then he put his nose against my nose and said, 'Did you hear me?'

"Then, somehow, I said something that made him laugh."

Forming a Relationship

Joby Wright's most trying days as a Hoosier came while he was sidelined awaiting NCAA permission to practice.

Wright's teammate, George McGinnis, had become a wealthy man by leaving school early and signing with the Indiana Pacers. Wright's thinking was, "If George can get a million dollars, maybe I can get at least a half-million."

Wright put his name on the draft lists of the National Basketball Association and the now defunct American Basketball

Association, knowing he had until a certain date to remove it from pro eligibility. Knowing Joby was in New York City, Knight tracked him down and had a talk.

"He said, 'You need to come back.' He talked to me in a manner where we connected. I was real impressed with the fact that he had tracked me down," Wright recalled. "I thought there was going to be a whole lot of hollering and screaming, but he was just talking. That set the tone for us to have a relationship through the years."

Wright said he wrote a letter to NBA officials removing his name from the list, but sent a telegram to the ABA, which the NCAA apparently considered improper.

"Well, the NCAA was trying to take my senior year away, so for the first two weeks of my senior year I couldn't practice with the team. They had me sweating blood," he said.

During that period, Knight stuck with Joby and the matter was cleared up.

"He could have said to hell with me. He hadn't recruited me. I was an asshole the first time I saw him, and he said, 'Come back and play.' Then when I got out there he said, 'I'm going to make you captain of the team.' I was ready to run through a wall for him," Wright said.

Do It by the Book

Knight didn't stand for the least bit of levity in his early practices. Everything was by the book and no one was to make any play, take any shot or make any pass that he might not be called upon to make in a game.

On one occasion, guard Dave Shepherd threw a behind-the-back pass during free-throw practice and promptly was thrown out of practice.

Chapter 2

Tales from Laz's Memory Bank

Laz First Cheered Against Hoosiers

My first memory of IU basketball was when my dad took me to my first Big Ten game. I believe it was in 1961. We were living in Cedar Rapids, Iowa, about a half-hour from Iowa City, and he comes home from work one day and has two tickets to the Big Ten game: Indiana vs. Iowa. I was kind of a basketball fan, shooting around the yard and stuff, and we get to this game at the old fieldhouse in Iowa City. The Hawkeyes come out to warm up and I stand up and start cheering for the Hawkeyes.

Well, my dad grabs me by the arm, sits me down and says, "Son, you're a Hoosier and you'll always be a Hoosier, no matter where we live." He grew up in South Bend and went to Central after John Wooden had been the coach there. Never played ball, wasn't an athlete, but knew what a Hoosier was.

Indiana won the game, and I was disappointed that Iowa, which I thought was my home team, had lost. But I learned a

Laskowski, being hoisted up after helping IU defeat Purdue late in the 1973-74 season. He played a big role in the team's Big Ten co-championship.
Photo courtesy of IU Archives

valuable lesson, and that's what it means to be a Hoosier. Even if you're transplanted you still believe in the Hoosiers.

[When the Laskowski family moved to Iowa, the family kept its modest home in South Bend, renting it in anticipation of the day they might return. That occurred in the fall of 1961, and in the spring of '71 Bob Knight visited and offered John a scholarship to play at Indiana.]

Laz a Star, But No All-Star

I didn't make the Indiana All-Star team that meets Kentucky every summer. It took many years, but I now suspect I know why.

My high school coach, Bob Donewald, talked to me in January of my senior year and said, "I know you're having a good year. You're averaging 29 points a game, sixth leading scorer in Indiana." Then he said, "You're not going to make the All-Star team."

I said, "What do you mean?" and he said again, "You're not going to make the Indiana All-Star team. I just want to tell you that now so you won't be thinking about it." Then he said, "I think we're going to be able to get you a scholarship, but you're not going to make the All-Star team." That was the last I heard of it.

Sure enough, they announce the team in May and I'm not on it. I had finished the year at 28.9 points. I was second-team All-State, as voted by the media. So I'm thinking I should be among the top 12.

Years later I think I figured out what happened. In those days, you didn't see the kids like you do now, so they counted on the college coaches in Kentucky and Indiana to help select the team. It sounds like a nice way to do it, but what I think happened was deals were being made with high school coaches. They'd promise if you send your kid to this school they would get your kid on the All-Star team. There's no other way my coach could have known in January that I wasn't going to make the team.

Laz Leaves for Bloomington

The recruiting trip was pretty interesting. I had only been on a plane one time and that was to fly back for my father's funeral. When IU recruited me, they put me on a flight from South Bend to Indianapolis on a five- or six-passenger plane. My ears blocked up on the up-and-down flight, and Coach came up to meet me with Bob Weltlich. Coach waited in the car, and I get out of the plane and there's Weltlich waiting for me. I don't know how he knew who I was, but he said, "I'm the assistant coach at Indiana."

We get in the car and Coach is driving. Weltlich is on the passenger side and I'm in the back seat. As soon as we get in the car, Coach starts the recruiting pitch. I remember driving through the limestone area and Coach explaining it, but I couldn't really hear what he was talking about. Not only did I have my ears plugged up from the flight, but he was talking into the windshield as he was driving.

I didn't say anything at all, half because I couldn't hear anything and half because I was so shy I wouldn't say anything. He must have thought I was the quietest, shyest kid in the world, but I didn't want to admit I couldn't hear what he was talking about.

Laskowski Was Down Recruiting List

Indiana was the only Big Ten school that offered me a scholarship, and that was because Coach Knight was looking for Indiana kids. I was a late bloomer in high school, and most of the guys had made up their minds where they wanted to go. I found out later that a six-foot-five guard-forward was what coach had in mind.

That fit my role, but the best at that role was Pete Trgovich from East Chicago Washington. This guy was the next Pete Maravich. He looked like Pete Maravich, played for an undefeated state champion. I mean, he was that guy.

I talked to Trgovich and he said Coach had come up and offered him a chance to come to Indiana but he was already headed to UCLA. Then Coach talked to Jerry Nichols of Greenwood, another six-five guard-forward who went to Purdue. I asked each of them if they had a chance to go to Indiana and they turned it down. I was the third choice at that position.

Green Hated Kentucky

Steve Green was a great shooter, a great competitor. His dad was his coach, so that gave him a great knowledge of the game. He knew he wanted to be a dentist, and he's not signed up but he's leaning to Vanderbilt when Coach Knight gets the Indiana job.

Here's a guy who hates Kentucky, grew up in Sellersburg and just hates Kentucky. He thought at Vanderbilt he could play against them. And now, there's a new coach at Indiana and he ends up coming to Indiana.

We both were shooters. We both lacked some defensive skills, had to work hard at it, but Steve was a great leader and a great go-to guy. When Scott May got hurt in the first half against Purdue, I think Steve got 15 or 20 points in the second half. He knew he had to take the load, and I remember him making shot after shot to pull it out. You're talking about one of the top shooters in Indiana history.

Flynn, Conner, Grevey and Ronnie Lyons

Being from South Bend, I really hadn't gotten into this Kentucky rivalry until we played a freshman game at Freedom Hall in Louisville. Kentucky had Mike Flynn, who was our Mr. Basketball, and Jimmy Dan Conner, who was Kentucky's. Their Kevin Grevey also had been Ohio's Mr. Basketball.

This was as big as it can get. Our game was the same night as Steve Downing scored 47 points for the varsity to help us beat Kentucky. We got down there and these Indiana fans were going crazy, and the Kentucky fans? Oh, my gosh!

They beat us in the freshman game, and then we didn't lose to them again until Dayton in 1975. When we went to Freedom Hall and beat Kentucky as juniors, it was as if the world had ended. We beat them in the NCAA regional at Vanderbilt in 1973 and beat them earlier that year in Bloomington. We beat them my junior year and beat them my senior year.

That game as a junior in Freedom Hall, they had a little redhead named Ronnie Lyons, who had been their Mr. Basketball and came from out in the hills of Kentucky. We had Buckner, Crews and myself as the guards, and Ronnie Lyons had to guard me because we had tall guards.

I'm looking at this guy and he's not even six feet. I had played center and forward in high school, and Coach is running a switch thing where I'm playing forward and Ronnie Lyons is guarding me. I thought, "This is easier than high school." I was able to play very well against Ronnie Lyons.

I've got a picture at home and I'm going in for a layup after stealing this pass. I'm jumping up and there's little Ronnie and he's not even close. I had this six-foot guy trying to stop me and I said, "Get me the ball." It was great.

Buckner had Wide Choice of Schools

The first time you met Quinn Buckner you knew he was a winner. I was a freshman when he was being recruited, and I was in the car with him and Coach Weltlich during his official visit.

Coach Weltlich asked him where else he was thinking of going, and he said he had visited UCLA and he had visited Michigan. He's reeling off all these powerhouses. Here I am, just a freshman from South Bend St. Joe and I'm trying to figure this thing out. The guy's talking about the dynasties of the time and I think,

"What am I doing here if this guy's thinking about coming to Indiana?"

But he came here, and you understood just by his actions and the way he carried himself that he knew what it took to win.

Quinn Played Two Sports

Quinn Buckner was a defensive back, and occasional offensive player, for two seasons on the Indiana football team. I think Coach Knight saw the importance that Buckner had to our team and that he was losing practice time until the beginning of December. We really started on October 15 in those days, and that represented a good five or six weeks where we didn't have him.

His freshman year we went to the Final Four in St. Louis and played UCLA with Quinn and Jim Crews, another freshman, as the guards. We saw how young that team was going to be and how important he was to us. We needed to mold that team from October 15, and I think that's how the conversation went down and Quinn decided to move on. Of course, we loved to have him because he was such a great leader.

May was Quiet...and Lethal

Scott May and Bobby Wilkerson came in one year after I did but were ineligible to play as freshmen until getting their academics in order. I had seen Bobby with the Indiana All-Star team, but I hadn't seen Scott play yet.

Scott and Bobby couldn't even practice with the team their first season. Instead, they would go down to the HPER Building and play in the rec leagues and that kind of stuff. I recall playing in some preseason pickup games, and Scott just had a sense about the things he could do. He was very quiet, not a vocal player at all, but a big, strong guy who was a great match for Steve Green. Steve and he could do some different things together and make

*Scott May was College Player of the Year after
leading Indiana to an unblemished record in 1976.
Photo courtesy of IU Archives*

up for the other's weaknesses. Coach liked Scott right from the start. He knew this guy could be a player, and it didn't take long for us to figure it out, either.

Scott wasn't a guy who really scored on his own. He waited for the pick and our offense was made for a guy coming off a screen. On the other hand, Green wasn't as good a defensive player, and May usually guarded the guy who had to be stopped. He was just the right guy to complement Green at the other forward.

1973 Hoosiers Rein in Gophers

Minnesota had a one-game lead on us with two games to go and they still had to play Iowa and Northwestern. Neither one of those teams was very good. We were off on Thursday and, sure enough, they got beat by Iowa and we were tied. If we could win on Saturday we would tie them for the Big Ten championship.

We beat Purdue in Assembly Hall and the game was over about four o'clock. The Minnesota game was later, and we heard that Northwestern had beaten Minnesota and we were the Big Ten champions. It wasn't on television, and this was before the days of *SportsCenter*. But somehow we heard that we won the Big Ten, and we were in shock that they lost two games at the end. In those days, the only way you could get in the NCAA Tournament was by being the conference champion.

You could tell that Minnesota was so much the better team. My sophomore year I was no match for Clyde Turner, Ron Behagen and Dave Winfield. These were men, and I was expected to go in there and battle those guys for rebounds. We lost to them in Minnesota that year and we'd always heard these stories about Coach Knight and how vicious the locker room talks were with stuff banging around. But the locker room door opened and he said, "Fellows, we played well today, but we didn't win the game. Let's get dressed and go home."

Hoosiers Sing St. Louis Blues

We reached the Final Four in 1973 after beating Marquette and Kentucky in Nashville, Tenn., and our semifinal opponent was UCLA, which had All-American Bill Walton. Don Noort was our backup center and we didn't have anybody to replicate Walton. So, Coach brings a tennis racket to practice and a manager would reach up with the tennis racket and that would be Bill Walton. That's what Steve Downing, our center, had to practice against.

Mentally, that was a tough game for me. Here I am a sophomore in college, not well recruited, watching UCLA win all those championships in the '60s. Lew Alcindor. Bill Walton. John Wooden. I mean, this was just a machine. When they beat Jacksonville with Artis Gilmore and Pembroke Burrows in 1970, I decided nobody was going to beat these guys. Ever.

Now it's three years later and there's John Wooden, and there's Bill Walton, and there's Keith Wilkes and all those guys. I'm thinking, "You're just a West Side Polish kid from South Bend. I mean, do you really belong here?" I remember I missed a bunch of shots and got only two points the whole game.

But Steve Downing was ready. He was a big-time player; the rest of us were just freshmen and sophomores and we were in awe of the place. We had two freshman guards, Jim Crews and Buckner. We've got two seniors, no juniors and these other guys. I mean, how do you get this team to the Final Four?

It wasn't as big then as it is now, but St. Louis Arena held 17,000 or 18,000 people and we were still nervous. UCLA beat us 70-59, and I really used that as a learning experience for the next year.

A foul call in the game was critical. Downing set up to take a charge and Walton had the ball. Downing had four fouls, and there was contact and the call went against Steve. His fifth foul and he was out. Walton also had four fouls, and we had staged a 17-0 run that had cut a 46-23 UCLA lead to three points. Downing outscored Walton 26-14, but an IU win wasn't to be.

A Quick-change Artist

We had those candy-striped pants for warmups, but in those days we didn't have the breakaway type and it took a while to get out of your pants. The last thing you wanted to do was not be ready to go in the game, because if you weren't ready when he wanted you, Coach would just as soon go to the next guy.

What I did after warmups would be to take my pants off, and as we sat on the bench I'd lay my pants on top of me so it would be as if I still had them on. So when he said, "Laz, get in there," whoosh, they were off. They were never on, but it looked as if they were.

Ice Cream for Everyone . . .

My junior year we played at Ohio State on Saturday and lost, which left us one game against Purdue to be co-champions with Michigan. Coach was very upset about losing to Ohio State, because had we won we would have been outright champs.

We went to practice Monday and he was very upset. He was watching the tape and he was mad at everybody. It was a tough practice, and Tuesday it was tougher. It seemed to be going downhill all week. He was not happy with us at all and we were a little ticked off at him, too. We showed up for practice on Friday and we'd only practiced about 10 minutes when he said, "That's enough."

We kind of trudged back to the locker room, and he had our chairs pulled out in front of our lockers with our game-day uniforms there. He said tomorrow's an important game and said there are a lot of Indiana basketball players who have never been in our shoes and had a chance to play for the Big Ten championship. He said they were all going to be watching the game on TV, and he said there were other Indiana players who were good players on very good teams but they never had a chance to play one game for the Big Ten championship. It was really a terrific talk about pulling ourselves out of the dumps that we were in.

*Coach Knight surprised the entire team by
serving ice cream sundaes after a tough loss.
Photo courtesy IU Archives*

We went back on the floor and looked across at the scorer's table, and sitting on the scorer's table appeared to be a two-gallon drum of vanilla ice cream. Twelve dishes. Twelve spoons. Chocolate sauce. Bananas. Cherries. I was a two-time All-Big Ten academic, so I was a little smarter than the other guys. I said, "Fellows, those are ice cream sundaes." And so 12 guys in their practice gear started dipping ice cream, and he said, "Practice is over."

I went back to the fraternity house and the guys there knew we were having a tough week and they said, "Ah, you got kicked off the team, didn't you?"

"No," I said, "you won't believe what happened." It completely changed the mental frame of mind that we were in... and the result was a victory.

Now we were playing Purdue, and I recall looking at that scoreboard with about 10 minutes to go. We were down 10 points and I was looking around at the guys thinking to myself, "Unless we come back and win this game there will never be ice cream again at an Indiana practice."

Well, we came back and got a three-point lead with a minute to go. Purdue cut it to one and Bruce Parkinson stole the ball and put them ahead. Quinn Buckner threw it to me and I looked at Bob Knight on the bench. I've got the greatest college coach in the country sitting on my bench. Surely, he's got a play figured out.

He never likes to call a timeout in that situation, so as I brought the ball up the court I took a look at him and all he did was give me a signal to bring the ball up the court. I thought, "Thanks, Coach. It's good to have you over there."

Somebody was going to have to take a game-winning shot, but the problem was we had no seniors on the floor. If you're a senior and take the game-winning shot and you miss it, your career's over, but when you're a junior and miss it you have to come back the next year and they boo you the whole season!

I took the shot and got it blocked. There was a scramble on the floor and Purdue fouled me. I made the first free throw and Purdue called a timeout. Coach sat us down and the first thing he told us was what we were going to do after I made this next free throw. He never said, "If he misses this is what we're going to do." I was an 80 percent foul shooter, but I was thinking about those two out of 10 that I would miss.

He showed confidence in me. The next free throw went in. Purdue got a shot off the baseline, but Steve Green, who had no jumping ability, blocked it and we won the game.

The Thing with Kentucky

In December of the 1974-75 season, Kentucky came into Assembly Hall and we won that game by 24 points. Absolutely killed them. We knew we were a better team than Kentucky. We had won six straight games after Scott May broke his arm at Purdue, so we were a pretty confident team as we prepared to play Kentucky again.

The rematch with Kentucky was in Dayton, Ohio, and we all wondered about this wrap Scott had on his arm. Would it fit the NCAA regulation and would it be soft enough for him to play? It was his left arm, but it still affected his shot. He started that game and went two or three minutes and you could tell it wasn't the same. So I came into the game right away.

Kentucky had a wonderful team, but I think the real key in our loss was us giving up 92 points. The final score was 92-90, and that was unheard of because we were a great defensive team. Something got into Kentucky offensively. They were just hot and then they banged around inside and really roughed up our guys.

During warmups the Kentucky players stopped when "My Old Kentucky Home" was played. They all lined up beyond the circle and stood at attention. I thought it was kind of goofy, because when you're warming up you're supposed to be thinking about the game. But mentally, they seemed to be ready to play and couldn't remember that we'd beaten them by 24 points. They were ready to go and it was nip and tuck all the way.

It was a tough locker room, because we didn't anticipate losing. We were on a roll. We were on our way to being an undefeated team, but it didn't work out.

Tough Places to Play

Minnesota was the toughest road trip in the Big Ten, along with Purdue and the rivalry we had with them. The physical presence at Williams Arena was different. Their guard, current Minnesota Timberwolves head coach Phil Saunders, would spin the ball on his finger and do "Sweet Georgia Brown" during warmups. That was to get the crowd going.

The hockey arena was in another part of the building. They had a video screen there, and fans paid money to watch the ballgame there. So there were more than 20,000 people in that big barn. They were absolutely wild about their Gopher team. It was very impressive to go in there, and that's why they were so hard to beat.

I heard a story that Bill Musselman would turn the heat off in Williams Arena on Friday night, and when we came in to warm up it'd be cold in there. I can't verify that, but it was a hotbed to play in.

Then they had Dave Winfield and those other big guys. Winfield was a good basketball player, but obviously he had a great baseball career. But just the imposing figure of those guys lining up and knowing you had to guard one of them made you shake a little bit.

Wins were Tough at Mackey

I told my son, Scott, that I wanted to take him to Purdue to see an IU game because it's so much different than coming to Assembly Hall. In Coach Davis's first year I finally took him. We came to the shootaround and rode over on the team bus and he got to sit on the floor and even shoot a basket. It was a game Indiana won, and you're never confident of winning a game at Mackey. He was a fourth grader at the time, and he still talks about how Indiana beat Purdue. It's that special when you beat Purdue.

Evolution of a Super Sub

In the fall of '75 I was a senior and Bobby Wilkerson was a junior. He was coming along after being ineligible his freshman year and playing a little bit as a sophomore, when he was still learning the system. In Bobby's junior year, Coach was trying to decide how to use him because he knew Buckner was a great guard, and if he puts Wilkerson in there he's got a guy who jumps center and plays guard defensively against everybody's best player.

He called me over to practice one day and said, "I've asked you to be a sub during your career here. I was a sub at Ohio State and I always wanted to start, but I never got the opportunity and that was important to me." He told me, "You've earned the right to start this year based on what you've done the last two years. If you want to start you let me know, and I think you and Buckner can be the starting guards."

But he also said he could see Wilkerson coming on, and I knew it was going to be important for him to start, too. What a great combination, and I'm filling in for whoever, so I said, "Coach, I'd just as soon keep it like it is. I'll come off the bench. I'm used to it. I know what to do, and I know what you want me to do. Go ahead with Wilkerson."

He was leaning toward that, but he wanted to talk to me about it, which was a great idea on his part. But what an athlete to have in there. Wilkerson didn't score a lot, but that wasn't what we needed. We had plenty of scorers. We had guys who loved to shoot.

*The lanky "super sub" heads up court after a steal. Laskowski
earned the right to start as a senior but agreed with coach
Knight that he could best help his team by coming off the bench.
Photo courtesy IU Archives*

Sub Could Study Flow of Game

What people didn't realize about the Super Sub label was what an advantage it was. I was not a great specimen on the floor. I was six feet five, 175 pounds, and to be able to sit on the bench for 10 minutes and see what was going on was beneficial. I could see the type of offense that was being run by other teams and see who was hot that day. I could even figure out whom I might replace, because if someone was in foul trouble or wasn't having a good game I could study his man. The other team was 10 minutes more tired than I was, because I was sitting on the bench and I knew I was the first guy in every time.

Knight Broke Up Guard Combination

Knight later thought he perhaps shouldn't have broken up the Buckner-Wilkerson combination that was so outstanding on defense. My insertion into the lineup during May's injury meant that Wilkerson moved to forward. Coach could have kept me as the sixth man and used Tom Abernethy at forward.

After Scott hurt his arm at Purdue, the team bused to Champaign to play Illinois on Monday and Coach was thinking about what to do. We went to practice Sunday and Coach said, "Laz, I'm going to start you on Monday. I want you to stay at the top of the key. They're going to play a zone defense and when the ball swings around I want you to take this shot from the top of the key. It's going to be open for you."

I practiced that shot on Sunday and Monday and started the game and, sure enough, they come out in that zone. The ball came around and I shot and made it. There were no three-pointers at the time. I averaged about 10 points a game for my career at Indiana and I got 18 points in the first half. Of course, any player who gets the green light loves it, and I got 10 more and set my career high that day with 28.

Bennie Bunks Down in Bloomington

Kent Benson was a critical recruit for the Hoosiers, who needed only a center to complete the blueprint for a dynasty in the mid-1970s. Bennie was such a fine prospect that when he visited Kentucky they sent a band out to the airport to welcome him.

One week before Benson's official visit to Indiana, I was at a Beach Boys concert at Notre Dame and saw him on his recruiting trip with a couple of Notre Dame players. We didn't have a concert where we could entertain him, but the next week on his IU visit, Steve Green showed him around and took him over to the Phi Gamma Delta fraternity house, where they didn't have a bed big enough for him.

Greeno, being the Plan B professional, just pulled the mattress off the bed, put it on the floor and Bennie got to sleep on the floor. Steve told him when he got here they'd have an extra long bed in his dorm room, but for now he was going to have to sleep on the floor.

I think Bennie understood that this was how IU was and he wanted to come to Indiana.

Benson Wanted to Quit Team

When he got here Bennie was the only freshman on the team, but he also was the only six-ten guy we had. We needed to have a center, so Coach was really on him to get going from day one. He was the missing part.

But Bennie really took it hard. He couldn't understand why he was getting picked on. Obviously, he was a star and had been the biggest kid around his whole life, and now things had changed.

I remember seeing him in the locker room after practice and he said, "Laz, I'm going to quit the team. I'm going to get in the car and drive back to New Castle. I just can't handle this." And I said, "Let me walk you back to your room."

We walked to McNutt Quad, a very short trip, and by the time we got there I'd convinced him that coach really liked him and the reason he was yelling at him was that we needed him on the team and he needed to do some things differently. I told him if he'd just stick it out everything would pay off.

He'd say, "All right, I'll stick it out," and then two weeks would go by and he'd say, "I'm quitting," and we'd do it all over again. I bet we did it three or four times, but each time he was able to come back, and I know today that he's glad he did.

Chapter 3

Great Hoosiers, Good Hoosiers and Memorable Hoosiers

Slim Bill from Shelbyville

Before Bill Garrett arrived in Bloomington, he already was one of the most celebrated players in Indiana. The six-foot-two African American had led Shelbyville to the 1947 Indiana high school basketball championship, an especially admirable feat because he outdueled 6'9" Clyde Lovellette of Terre Haute Garfield in the championship game.

Lovellette would go on to lead Kansas to the 1952 NCAA championship while averaging 28.4 points a game and become a longtime player in the National Basketball Association.

"Here was Lovellette, six-nine, big and burly, and Garrett was six-two and very slightly built, and Garrett just ate him up. Just ate him up," former IU sports information director Tom Miller recalled.

Garrett's roommate, Bill Tosheff, described him as being "quietly lethal."

"He wouldn't say too much, but boy, could he fly. He worked as a center in the system, but we were always in transition, the Hurryin' Hoosiers. I would say, 'If they score on us you take off,'" Tosheff recalled. "He was a low-hurdles champion, and I'd throw a football pass to him and he'd score in about three seconds."

Garrett would become an All-American with the Hoosiers, averaging 13 points a game in 1949-50. More memorable, however, was the fact that he became the first African-American standout in the Big Ten.

"I think during the war years Iowa might have had a black player on its squad, but I don't know how much he played," Miller said. "It ultimately came down to Branch McCracken's decision on whether we take a black."

A year earlier Anderson's Johnny Wilson, also an African American, had led his team to the Indiana high school championship. According to Miller, McCracken took some heat for not recruiting Wilson.

"Branch wasn't sure that this was the time yet, and he thought about it a long time," Miller said.

Shelbyville insurance man Nate Kaufman took a special interest in Garrett and approached IU's esteemed president Herman B Wells about the Shelbyville star playing for the Hoosiers. Wells already was leading a campaign to bring down barriers faced by blacks on the Bloomington campus.

Wells later recalled that a trend of thinking in that day claimed that basketball was too much of a contact sport for the various races to mix on the court. IU athletic director Zora Clevenger was concerned that the presence of a black player might cause scheduling difficulties, but ultimately, he left the decision up to McCracken. Branch had some concerns, but Wells's feelings were strong, and the IU president said he would take the responsibility for any backlash.

As it turned out, any concerns were groundless.

"Bill was a nice, uncomplicated kid. I don't think he thought of himself as being black and he got along with everybody. He never was a problem," Miller said.

Garrett went on to play for the Harlem Globetrotters and coached Indianapolis Crispus Attucks to the 1959 Indiana high school championship.

In 1974, one day after Bill and Betty Garrett's 32nd wedding anniversary, Garrett told his wife he loved her and headed for an Indianapolis discount store to get a replacement for a broken window. As he stood in a checkout line, the former Hoosier collapsed. He died four days later from heart faliure.

Kokomo's Splendid Splinter

Indiana basketball thrives on legends, and when Jimmy Rayl arrived at the IU campus in the fall of 1959 he already was one. The Splendid Splinter had led Kokomo to the championship game of the '59 Indiana state tournament and established a reputation as perhaps the best outside shooter in Indiana high school history.

Rayl was a player to whom many Hoosier teenagers could relate. At six feet two and about 150 pounds, he could have been mistaken for almost any Indiana farm boy. By the time he left Bloomington he had produced the two biggest outbursts in IU history, 56-point games against Minnesota in 1962 and Michigan State in '63. He also had 44 against Michigan State and Wisconsin, 41 against DePaul and 37 against Michigan, Illinois and Purdue.

But the legend of Jimmy Rayl was founded upon a high school game in New Castle, Ind., in 1959. It was played in a tiny gym that held only about 1,800 and was packed to the rafters. A short time later the New Castle Trojans would move into the largest high school gym in the nation, a building in which two other IU stars, Kent Benson and Steve Alford, would be weaned as prolific scorers.

The game will be remembered as the night New Castle's Ray Pavy, later to become Rayl's teammate at Indiana, scored 51 points while Jimmy was good for 49. But the game was much more than that.

*Ray Pavy outdueled Jimmy Rayl 51-49 in a high school game,
but a paralyzing traffic accident abruptly ended his career.
Photo courtesy of IU Archives*

Both schools were members of the North Central Conference, easily the strongest and most recognizable group of schools in Indiana basketball. Muncie Central, now with eight state championships, was the centerpiece of the league. Kokomo, which would win its only state crown two years later, Marion, now with six championships, and Lafayette Jefferson, with three, were others. Anderson, with its famous arena, The Wigwam, was another member.

New Castle and Kokomo were challenging for the NCC championship in the final game of the '59 season. New Castle won 92-81 as Pavy, No. 23, matched Rayl, No. 32, shot for shot. Pavy, later paralyzed by an auto accident during his undergraduate days, made 23 of 38 shots and Rayl hit 18 of 33.

One game earlier, Rayl had scored 48 and averaged 40 over his last six regular-season games. Then, in a classic Fort Wayne semi-state match against another future IU teammate, Tom Bolyard, Rayl scored 40 to Bolyard's 34 and hit a midcourt bomb in the last second as Kokomo beat Fort Wayne South 92-90.

"It just seemed like it was back and forth," Rayl said of the faceoff with Pavy. "He got a lot of layups driving for the basket and most of mine were from outside."

Rayl still delights in the fact that he won one duel with Pavy that night.

"Back then, if you led the North Central Conference in scoring, it was a pretty big deal. I had won it my junior year and I went into this game, the last game of the season, 10 points ahead of Ray. Ray got 51 and I got 49, so I won by eight. I was glad he outscored me, looking back on it."

Pavy was paralyzed in September of 1961 when he was involved in a traffic accident near Fowler, Ind. His fiancee, Betty Sue Pierce of New Castle, was killed.

"You Can't Blame Yourself"

More than four decades after Pavy's tragic accident, the one-time New Castle star attended a Bloomington banquet honoring the school's All-Century team. As Pavy sat in his wheelchair, former roommate Gary Long pushed him around the buffet table.

Over the years Long has thought many times about how Pavy could have avoided his horrible accident. The same night as Pavy's crash Long was holding a rehearsal dinner for his wedding the next day. He had thought about including his roommate in the wedding party, but had stuck almost strictly with relatives in naming his attendants.

"Of course, you can't blame yourself, but I almost had him as the best man in my wedding," Gary said. "It was a Friday night and he was on his way to another fraternity brother's wedding. If I had had him in the wedding party he wouldn't have been heading where he was heading. If I'd gone ahead and done that . . . and I came really close to doing it."

A Career That Wasn't Fulfilled

Pavy played only one season with the Hoosiers, averaging 2.5 points a game as a sophomore, but his ex-roommate believes he would have had a solid career.

"He would have been a great player just because of his common sense," Long said. "He wasn't as quick as you probably need to be. He had great big legs, but Larry Bird proved you don't have to be super quick, and I think Ray would have been a Larry Bird type of player. He had a court sense."

Long said Pavy would have been a great team leader.

"It's just a shame. I never did see Ray get down. I went to see him right after the accident and we still didn't know if he was going to live or die. He was on this big thing that stretched his spine out and he was joking then," Long said. "He was always a positive person. I was probably the closest person to him, and I never saw him complain or get down about anything."

The Dick and Tom Show

Twins hold a special place in the hearts of Indiana high school basketball fans. The most famous probably were Harley and Arley Andrews, who along with their uncle, Harold Andrews, helped Terre Haute Gerstmeyer reach the championship game of the 1953 state tournament. But the best twins were Dick and Tom Van Arsdale, who came to Indiana from Indianapolis Manual in 1961.

The pair was even more alike in talent than in appearance. In three seasons with the Hoosiers, Tom scored 1,252 points and Dick tallied 1,240. Tom averaged 17.4 points, Dick 17. As juniors Dick averaged 22.3 and Tom 21.3.

The Van Arsdales shared the Indiana High School Athletic Association's Trester Award and were co-recipients of the state's Mr. Basketball honor.

A sportswriting friend of Bob Knight first told him about the Vans, who were strong and quick forwards.

"Dick Otte told me that they'd start on opposite sides of the lane and knock people over until they met in the middle," Knight said.

While the twins always had played together through high school and college, both realized they would profit from going to different professional teams. Dick went to the New York Knicks, earning a starting role before being taken by Phoenix in the 1968 expansion draft. He earned three visits to the NBA All-Star Game and was the Suns' captain for eight years.

Tom enjoyed a 12-year career that saw him play in Cincinnati, Kansas City, Philadelphia, Atlanta and Phoenix. He also was an All-Star three times and was captain of the Cincinnati Royals. But, unlike Dick, he never played for a pro team with a winning record.

"They were really nice guys, but it was easy to recognize which one was which," teammate Jimmy Rayl said. "They weren't that identical once you were around them."

Dick (left) and Tom Van Arsdale were identical twins with identical skills.
Photo courtesy of IU Archives

George, We Hardly Knew Ye

George McGinnis may have turned more heads than any Hoosier of any era. He arrived in Bloomington at six feet seven and 235 pounds. His hands were as big as doormats and as soft as pillows, and his physique was virtually unequalled in the early 1970s.

Indiana has produced only a few players who excited coaches as much as George McGinnis. Maybe Rick Mount or Larry Bird. Certainly Oscar Robertson, but not many others. Along with fellow IU teammate Steve Downing, George led Indianapolis Washington to an unbeaten season and the 1969 state championship. His legend grew in the summer All-Star games against Kentucky when he scored 53 points against Kentucky All-Star Joe Voskuhl, who the prior week proclaimed him "not so tough."

Expectations for McGinnis only escalated as he sat out his freshman season, a requirement of that day.

"He is physically the most talented ballplayer that I've ever seen in the Big Ten," Northwestern coach Brad Snyder said.

"The man is big enough to go bear hunting with a buggy whip," added Ohio State's Fred Taylor.

It took McGinnis three seconds to score his first college basket, and he quickly became a legend around the Big Ten. Playing Northern Illinois in the middle of the Big Ten season, the Hoosiers escaped with a 113-112 victory in which McGinnis had 45 points and 20 rebounds. Downing contributed 17 points and 14 rebounds as the two former high school teammates combined for 64 points and made 26 of 46 shots.

"That McGinnis is some mean cat," said Northern Illinois forward Cleveland Ivey, who tried to guard him.

Former Ohio State player Don DeVoe, later a successful college coach, also heaped praise on the Indiana forward, saying, "I guarded Cazzie [Russell] when I played, but I'll guarantee you that I want no part of McGinnis."

"He looks like an unemployed blacksmith," added Michigan State coach Gus Ganakas.

George's high school football coach, Bob Springer, stated the obvious, "George could have been just as good in football as he was in basketball."

When Indiana played Michigan State, it was hard to tell which sport was being played. The Spartans had an All-America linebacker named Brad VanPelt, who would become a star with the New York Giants. Indiana won the first meeting in East Lansing as McGinnis scored 24.

Ganakas, probably unintentionally, took a slam at IU football by telling Indiana writers, "That probably was the best football game *your* people have seen for a long time."

"The rematch was seven days later in Bloomington, and despite physical defending by VanPelt, McGinnis scored 37 points and made 15 of 28 shots. VanPelt scored 13 and was victimized by George's 25 second-half points in the Hoosiers' 90-76 win.

"Some of the things he does should be outlawed," Ganakas said as a compliment.

"That was a sample of what that guy can do when he gets fired up," VanPelt said.

In George's first three Big Ten games he averaged 35.3 points and 21.7 rebounds.

McGinnis and Downing, whom Bob Knight said probably represented the best tandem to come from the same high school team, had an incredible outburst in an 88-79 victory at Illinois on Feb. 20. George had 33 points and 15 rebounds, while Downing produced 28 points, 17 rebounds and 10 blocked shots.

By the way, McGinnis played only 27 minutes in the game.

McGinnis never played for Knight, turning professional with the Indiana Pacers after his sophomore season. McGinnis always said the arrival of the discipline-minded new coach didn't affect his decision, but many IU fans pondered what IU's Final Four team might have done with George present in 1973.

"I've never seen a man so massive who could dribble the ball," former IU teammate Joby Wright said.

"George had to be one of the greatest players that ever played the game. George was an unbelievable talent."

As McGinnis prepared for a pro career, Louisville *Courier-Journal* sportswriter Dave Kindred asked him, "How good can you be, George?"

"From what they say, *awfully* good," he replied.

Always Secondhand Steve

Steve Downing, the six-foot-nine product of Indianapolis Washington High, always played in the shadow of prep teammate McGinnis.

Joby Wright, a teammate at IU, said the Downing who led Bob Knight's second team to the Final four wasn't the same player who came to Bloomington under Lou Watson.

"Downing got injured. I swear when Steve was a freshman, before he got hurt, he could almost touch the top of the backboard," Wright said. "Steve could jump. Steve Downing could jump out of the gym. What we saw of Downing his junior and senior years was not what we saw as a freshman and sophomore. Steve could jump six to eight inches higher then and he was a much better shot blocker and rebounder his first two years."

Downing, a longtime associate athletic director at Indiana before taking a similar position at Texas Tech, became one of Wright's closest friends over the years.

"Steve was so soft-spoken and such a gentleman. You never thought he could be as tough as he was on the floor," Joby said. "Off the floor, Steve was one of the nicest human beings. In my mind he compares with Willis Reed, who is so soft-spoken, so nice and such a gentle guy until he goes on the floor. Steve was like that. Off the floor he was so soft-spoken, but on the court he would block shots and rebound the ball with a vengeance."

Downing played in the massive shadow of McGinnis at Washington and during their sophomore seasons in Bloomington, a shadow that Downing escaped when George turned pro early.

"George was always considered the better player, no question," Wright said, "but Steve was a valuable asset and I don't think Steve ever got the credit he deserved."

*Steve Downing showed his true worth after high school teammate
George McGinnis turned pro after their sophomore season. Downing
grabbed 26 rebounds in the first game played in the Assembly Hall.
Photo courtesy IU Archives*

The Day the World Turned

In June of 1982 the Boston Celtics peaked during their NBA draft by selecting a 6'10" kid out of Indiana whose potential had reversed itself in an horrific traffic accident the previous summer. Landon Turner, whose surge near the end of the 1980-81 season was considered the major thrust in Indiana winning its fourth NCAA championship, welcomed the Celtics' thoughtfulness by saying, "You made my day. When do I report?" The Celtics' pick was a gesture of goodwill only, as they drafted him knowing he would not be able to play professionally.

Until July 25, 1981, a fateful Saturday when Turner and some friends decided to go to the King's Island amusement park near Cincinnati, he was looking forward to a senior season that might have seen him become a first-round draft pick. The accident occurred on Ind. 46, a curving two-lane highway between the Indiana cities of Columbus and Greensburg. The vehicle was a 1975 Ford LTD, a car large enough to offer a little head room to the former Indianapolis Tech star.

After the crash on a curve that later was improved by highway construction, Turner has spent most of his life in a two-wheel vehicle, and every time his wheelchair moved onto the floor at Assembly Hall Landon was reminded of the love affair between IU fans and former players.

At the time Bob Knight was in Idaho deliberating whether to take a commentator's job with CBS Sports. Turner and his coach had endured a checkered relationship because of Landon's on-again, off-again play and effort. For a time Turner appeared to be a man without a focus, as misdirected in the classroom as he was on the court. But when the lanky Hoosier got his act straight he represented one of Knight's proudest moments.

Turner's dilemma may have convinced the coach to stay away from television. Knight founded the Landon Turner Trust Fund and became one of his most diligent supporters. Furthermore, Knight tried to make Landon feel a part of the team, even asking him to shave off a mustache that violated the Hoosiers' no-facial-hair rule.

Turner's spinal cord injuries curtailed his basketball career, except for his play on a wheelchair team in the late 1980s. Eight years after his accident Turner was awarded the Most Courageous Award by the U.S. Basketball Writers Association.

The group's president, Malcolm Moran, said, "This is not about what he was. This is about what he is."

Stevie Wonder: The Perfect Hoosier

Most Indiana schoolboys have a dirt court alongside the barn to shoot baskets, but Steve Alford had the world's "largest, finest" high school gymnasium. The son of Sam Alford, a prep coach who had starred at Franklin College, Steve could shoot almost any time he wanted in the fieldhouse at New Castle High, for whom he scored 57 points in a 1983 semi-state game.

Good things happened swiftly for Alford once he arrived at Indiana University. As a freshman he scored 27 points as the Hoosiers posted a 72-68 victory over No. 1 North Carolina in the 1984 Sweet Sixteen. That summer he would be a starting guard on the U.S. Olympic team some believe was the finest ever.

"He's not big. He's not strong. He's not quick, and it's hard for me to imagine how a kid like that scores so many points," coach Bob Knight said. "He can't post up. He can't really take it to the basket and he doesn't get rebound baskets. For a kid who only has a jump shot, he's as good a scorer as I've ever seen."

Alford, reared in Martinsville and New Castle, was a Hoosier from the get-go. As a junior he was eating lunch in the school cafeteria when his father came down and said that Knight had called and wanted him to play at Indiana.

"Well, if they want me, I want them," he said, and never considered going elsewhere.

As a senior at IU, Alford was receiving 150 fan letters a day and trying to answer them all. He answered a doorbell in the middle of the night once and found an adult with a basketball to be signed.

Alford was so popular that one New Castle woman taught her parakeet to say, "Ahhhh. Go, Stevie."

Calbert's Mother a Big Influence

Calbert Cheaney, the all-time Big Ten scoring champion, nearly attended the University of Evansville, where former IU guard Jim Crews was coach at the time. A graduate of Evansville Harrison High, Cheaney missed much of his senior season with a broken ankle and was largely unknown by many of the recruiting gurus.

"The only people who knew he was any good were his high school coach and me," Crews said later.

During the summer of 1988 Cheaney was leaning toward accepting an offer from the Purple Aces, but his mother, Gwendolyn, urged him not to rush his decision. Cheaney had such respect for his mother that he wasn't about to disregard her advice.

In fact, Cheaney's high school coach, Jerrill Vandeventer, said Calbert's mother cast a certain fear over his own life.

"Most of us are afraid of her. I think probably we both still are, fearing that Calbert would not meet her expectations in the classroom or whatever and suffer the consequences of not getting to play," Vandeventer said after Calbert became the 1993 National Player of the Year.

Bob Knight had witnessed Cheaney in one of his poorer games, so the former IU coach was cautious at first. When he got serious about wooing Calbert, Gwendolyn was a formidable obstacle.

"I didn't like him at first. I told him that," she said. "I was a hard person. I was asking everything. I asked him why he was such a hard person and he told me about himself, that his parents were disciplinarians, too. They weren't as hard as he was, but they were strong parents."

*IU picked up left-handed Calbert Cheaney, who went on to
become the Big Ten's all-time scoring leader, out of Evansville.
Photo courtesy IU Athletics*

A rating of that season's top 25 high school players by *The Courier-Journal* of Louisville, Ky., rated Cheaney between 10th and 15th in the nation. The publisher of one well-known recruiting service approached the reporter who had made the selections and said, "You've got Cheaney rated way too high. Way too high."

"He didn't get a lot of the publicity that a lot of other guys got, but he worked so hard," former teammate Chris Reynolds said. "When we came in we had a lot of guys who were *Parade* All-Americans and McDonald's All-Americans. I hadn't really heard of Calbert. I think my name was ahead of Calbert's on the All-America list in high school."

Cheaney, who went on to become the Big Ten's all-time scoring leader, didn't disagree.

"I didn't think I fit in. I didn't get as much notoriety as they did. All I heard about was Greg and Pat Graham and [Lawrence] Funderburke and Reynolds," Cheaney told *The Washington Post*, referring to classmates. "I'd seen them on Scholastic Sports America and everything. Coming in I really didn't think I had enough skill to play with players like that."

Shortly after the recruits arrived on campus, Reynolds noticed something about his new friend from Evansville.

"We played pickup games, and Calbert just seemed to hit all his shots," he said.

Bailey Had His Own Time Zone

The sign near the intersection of State Roads 446 and 58 reads: "Heltonville, Proud Home of Damon Bailey." It was erected more than a decade ago and has remained long after Bailey's basketball career ended.

Heltonville (population 500) is typical small-town Indiana. It is separated from Bloomington by 20 miles of curving two-lane highway and the state's largest body of water, Lake Monroe. When Bailey migrated north to play basketball for the Hoosiers, it is assumed that he walked across the lake.

Teammate Greg Graham, a more stylish city slicker from the east side of Indianapolis, once said that Damon had a "farm butt."

Bailey was never the best player in Indiana history, but he was the highest scorer and the most celebrated. Starting with Bob Knight raving about him when he was an eighth grader, Bailey went on to lead Bedford North Lawrence to a state championship before a packed Hoosier Dome crowd of about 40,000. His teams went 99-11 over four seasons. He was a folk hero at 14 and an icon at 18. One student teacher assigned to a Bedford-area school asked her supervisor how long she had been teaching there. The teacher replied, "I started when Damon was in the third grade."

The student aide was flabbergasted. "Everybody down there thinks in Damon Time," she said.

Bailey's four-year average at Indiana was a modest 13.2. However, Bailey wasn't judged by his jump shot but by other intangibles. He was no Brad Pitt physically. He was an unpretentious Hoosier with a modest ego, modest speed, modest leaping ability and a reputation as widespread as a spring flood.

Jimmy Chitwood, the star of *Hoosiers*, looked a bit nerdy, but Damon Bailey had Hoosiers written all over his six-foot-three, 200-pound body. The Indiana guard was so popular that one Indiana mother named her firstborn boy Damon and her firstborn girl Bailey. A woman two weeks shy of her 100th birthday asked to be taken from her nursing home so she could meet Bailey. One man went to meet Damon with his dog, named General Bailey in honor of Knight and Bailey.

All this for a man who was the 44th pick in the 1994 NBA draft and who failed to have a career of note as a professional.

Andrae the (Gentle) Giant

Bob Knight always preferred that his players have some fire in their bellies, but he made an exception when a handsome six-foot-nine, 235-pound military brat named Andrae Patterson became interested in attending Indiana. He was a McDonald's All-

*Soft-spoken Andrae Patterson had a masterful singing voice,
but his demeanor was a challenge for Coach Knight.
Photo courtesy IU Athletics*

American, seemingly cut from the same cloth as his All-Star team-mates, Antoine Walker of Kentucky and Jerod Ward of Michigan.

Van Coleman, a noted recruiting analyst, said Patterson might be Indiana's most athletic inside player since George McGinnis. Andrae was the ringleader of a well-recruited class including Charlie Miller, Neil Reed, Rob Hodgson and Michael Hermon. However, Hodgson transferred during his redshirt season, Hermon was dismissed from the team that year and Reed was asked to leave, later becoming a central figure in the ouster of Knight as coach.

Even before arriving on campus, Patterson said he wanted a coach like Knight.

"I want a coach that's going to yell at me and get me going. It will help me in the long run," Patterson said.

Sadly, it may not have.

Knight did plenty of yelling, but Andrae's career fell somewhat short of what the coach had anticipated. As a sophomore he went through 17 games in which he scored fewer than five field goals.

Patterson did erupt for 39 points against Duke as Indiana won the 1996 Preseason National Invitation Tournament at Madison Square Garden. Patterson had a strong finish to his senior year and enjoyed a short NBA career, but Knight always claimed he was a victim of a docile personality. Knight said Patterson always had a sensitive side that was trying to compete with the athletic part.

Current coach Mike Davis was an assistant during Patterson's senior season.

"I would have loved to have coached him. He was a talent," Davis said. "You look at him and [Jared] Jeffries and what was the difference? Jared maybe was a couple inches taller but, boy, Andrae just wanted someone to put an arm around him."

Recognizing that Andrae had a hot finish to his career, Davis said, "He did, but he could have been playing that way all the while. It was a shame he couldn't handle it. He took everything personally."

Dane Fife: IU's R-Rated Defender

Dane Fife brought combativeness to Indiana basketball that few Hoosiers have matched. The 6'4" son of a Michigan high school coach was first attracted to IU by the movie *Hoosiers*. His brother, Dugan, had played at Michigan and his father, Dan, had been an assistant coach there. A McDonald's All-American, Dane came to Bloomington with the grandiose goal of winning a national championship.

It almost happened in 2002, largely because Fife offered unique leadership. He had mediocre speed but an uncanny knack of not only playing great defense but getting into the head of the guy he was guarding.

Fife may have set a school record for trash talking.

"All I can say is that it was relentless," IU assistant coach Jim Thomas said. "He did it all the time. He took no breaks, whether it was in practice or not. I really respected him, because if he did that in practice I didn't expect him to do it any less in a game."

Added Mike Davis, "No matter who it was, he was going to say something. He had to have the last word."

Trash talker or not, Fife was one tough Hoosier. Once, he intentionally bit Iowa's Duez Henderson. He also once shaved his head, which led teammate Kyle Hornsby to say he looked like a rat.

"I may look like a rat, but I'm a tough rat," Dane countered.

Davis said he was bothered by his wife's comparison of her husband and Fife.

"I wasn't that way," the coach said. "Fife would get under people's skin. I got under people's skin but it was a clean version. Fife is like an R-rated version. He's gonna grab you. Pinch you. Hold you. Talk to you. Everything."

However, the coach said Dane never tried to pick a fight. His lone goal was to get an opponent off his game.

One of Fife's trademarks, visible even to fans, was that he had to have the last word.

*Dane Fife won over Hoosier fans and got under the skin of
opponents with a gritty, talkative style that made him an
unsung hero of IU's drive to the 2002 Final Four.
Photo courtesy IU Athletics*

"Fife was never wrong about anything," Davis said. "He always had an answer. You couldn't explain it to him without him saying or thinking, 'You're out of your mind.' Once he did that I'd just put him on the bench and say, 'Okay, I don't want to talk to you any more.'"

The coach said Fife's demeanor always changed when he was benched because he wanted to be on the floor.

"He would always act like he'd never done anything wrong," Jim Thomas continued. "He always kept you scratching your head. As a player I found he was the epitome of a guy who was a warrior. He probably wasn't the most athletic player I've been around, but he was probably the most determined guy."

Coverdale Could Rise to Occasion

Red-headed IU guard Tom Coverdale has been compared to Huck Finn and Opie Taylor—as well as to Dane Fife. Both Fife and Coverdale enjoyed only moderate foot speed. Both were aggressive defenders, and both worked to get under the skin of opponents.

However, Jim Thomas said Cov's trash-talking was a lot different from his former running mate's.

"He had a different style. He didn't go out aggressively talking it, but if you get him engaged in it you could wind up elevating his game because he didn't back down. He's in the same mold as Fife, but Cov kind of gradually got into it. If you wanted to engage him in it he didn't back down."

Coverdale came out of Noblesville High as the state's Mr. Basketball but was sent to New Hampton Prep School in New Hampshire for a year of seasoning. When he returned he played only 41 minutes as a freshman.

At the time, Indiana's backcourt was well stocked with A. J. Guyton and Michael Lewis, but Davis, then an assistant, could see evidence of Coverdale's potential.

"We had some really good stars, but one thing I noticed about Coverdale was that he never wanted to come out of practice. He wanted to play against A. J. and those guys. Sometimes you wanted to get him to the side of the court so other guys could participate, but he always wanted to play. That should have been a sign," Davis said.

Jim Thomas said the only similarities between Coverdale and Fife were their toughness and competitiveness.

"If another person was bigger or more athletic, that didn't phase them. Coverdale is more of a casual personality, and as a player he tended to carry that sometimes, but deep down he's competitive," the assistant coach said.

Chapter 4

Common Threads that Bind Hoosiers

Long's Son Played Buddy in Hoosiers

Brad Long, the oldest son of former Indiana guard Gary Long, was one of the stars of the movie *Hoosiers*. He played the gum-chewing, cocky player named Buddy (Number 14) in the mid-1980s movie that since has become a classic. Buddy was the player who got kicked off the Hickory team during coach Norman Dale's first practice but, inexplicably, was back on the team later in the movie.

"Our friends have said, 'How did Brad get back on the team?' Most people don't even notice it," said Gary, reviewing how a five-man roster at the start of practice grows to a more workable number. Much fanfare was made of Jimmy Chitwood's decision to rejoin the Huskers, but Buddy simply winds up on the roster again.

"Brad might be an actor right now if this hadn't happened," his father theorized. "He had a two-minute scene with Gene Hackman [portraying Coach Dale] where he drives up, goes into the bar and gives a big apologetic scene. We saw the uncut version and Gene Hackman told him, 'You did a great job.'"

But that scene wound up on the cutting-room floor along with around two hours of additional film that was shot and not used.

"It was the very last scene cut out. The director didn't like it but he didn't have control," Long said. "There was some confusion as to who Brad was at that stage of the movie. Some people thought he was Jimmy, the kid that didn't go out for the team."

Brad Long played basketball at Center Grove, near Indianapolis, and at Southwestern College in Winfield, Kansas, where his team went 18-1 and he made academic All-American. Although he was 22 years old, about two years older than the maximum age sought by the casting director, he decided to try out for the part.

"I don't know why, because he'd never done any acting except Jacob Marley in Scrooge," his father said. "He kept getting through the cuts. They were looking for players first and they wanted a certain type of character for each part. Brad wasn't a bad kid, but he kind of looked cocky to me when he played. He'd always do things on the court that I would kind of get on him about. They were looking for that kind of character."

Gary said they went through several thousand candidates before picking Brad for the part.

Gary revealed several things that wound up on the cutting-room floor, including the fact that George, the man trying to get Norman Dale fired, was supposed to be Buddy's father. The original idea called for two brothers to play on the team and for one of the cheerleaders to be Buddy's girlfriend.

"All of this was supposed to be in the movie, but none of it came out," Gary said.

Dad Also Gets a Part in Movie

When Gary Long, a graduate in 1961, played for IU he allowed an unknown youngster to rebound for him during a shooting practice. Almost 25 years later the small favor was returned.

The boy was Angelo Pizza, a Bloomington resident who wrote the movie *Hoosiers*.

"When he found out that Brad was my son he told him to get his dad," Gary said. "I guess I was a big hero to him and he said I was real nice to him. Anyway, he told Brad to get his dad and he'd give him a coach's part. They couldn't get a hold of me all day, and anybody could have come out of the crowd and would have loved to do it," Long said, "but it took four days to find me for that little part and you don't even see me."

Although his name appears in the movie's credits, Gary Long is barely distinguishable as the opposing coach in the regional final. However, he has good memories of pleasant conversations with stars Hackman and Barbara Hershey on the set.

Long was supposed to have had three words in the movie, but that opportunity vanished when he left the bench and headed for the scorer's table during the shooting. The scene involved Hickory's smallest player, Ollie, attempting two critical free throws near the end of the game.

Gary had a line in the script: "Foul the runt!"

"That was my line—foul the runt. My wife claims I went around the house practicing. I was supposed to have had a closeup and everything," he said. "The reason you don't see me is I kind of ran to the scorer's bench and said, 'Foul the runt.' Well, it turns out they had set up the scene for me to be sitting on the bench. I disappear and they dub in, 'Foul him.' The assistant coach says, 'Foul him.' They just told me to act like a coach. They didn't tell me to stay on the bench."

Those three little words could have brought Long money if not necessarily fame.

"If you have one line in a movie they have to pay you like an actor," he said. "I'd be in the Screen Actors Guild and everything.

Most people would have loved to do it for nothing and I was to get like $370 a day, plus overtime and then get royalties on the movie. It's unbelievable what it means to get a line in a movie."

Old Standards Finally Change

One of the old traditions of Indiana basketball died following the 2000-01 season when the double-armed basket standards in Assembly Hall were replaced with the more modern collapsible ones.

Safety was one factor in the change, but the old standards' lack of mobility was another.

"We changed them because we had great difficulty moving them," associate athletic director Chuck Crabb said. "There was, basically, one ton of pig iron on the back and, still, the most intense dunker could move the basket. The new goal supports are significantly easier to move and install."

Contrary to many thoughts, the change in head coaches in 2000 had nothing to do with the switch—although Bob Knight's departure did open the door. Crabb said athletic department officials had discussed making the change with Knight, but only briefly.

"There were approaches I made to Coach Knight—picking my moment—where I said we'd like to consider updating the standards," Crabb said. "He'd always look at me and his comment, with that little gleam in his eye, would be, 'Well, Chuck, have your standards won any national championships for Indiana University?'"

Crabb, of course, replied that they hadn't.

"Well, the ones that I have have had three national championships. So I don't think we're going to change, are we?" the coach countered.

"And I'd just say, 'No, Coach, we're not going to change,'" Crabb said.

Best Seat in the House

One could argue that Chuck Crabb has the best seat in Assembly Hall and possibly the best job.

"My dad always said, 'What more could you want? You do the announcing and you've got the cheerleaders,'" said the IU public address man, who has been an adviser to the IU cheer corps.

Crabb's team introduction—*Ladies and gentlemen, your Indiana Hoooosieeeerrs*—is one of the state's most recognizable phrases. From his seat near the left end of the scorer's table, Crabb has heard most of the remarks made between the Indiana coaches and officials.

"There have been interesting times. There was the UTEP game where Don Haskins wasn't too happy with how badly his team was getting beat by Indiana in the Indiana Classic championship game," said Crabb, referring to the Hoosiers' 75-43 victory in 1978-79. "There were moments when Coach Knight also was a little concerned with how his team was being treated, but he came over and the two big men sat on the table right in front of me. Knight gives Haskins a peppermint and starts talking about fishing in New Mexico."

Knight usually carried pieces of peppermint or butterscotch candy, often mouthing it during postgame press conferences as well as during the games.

"There was an IU-Purdue game before the coaches' boxes became the rule," Crabb said. "The two coaches actually crossed at center court and Knight was in front of Purdue's bench coaching his team and Gene Keady was almost in front of the Indiana bench coaching his team. And Knight gave Keady a piece of butterscotch as they walked back."

From his courtside seat, public address announcer
Chuck Crabb has overheard many interesting discussions.
Photo courtesy IU Archives

The Best-Laid Plans

The home team's locker room in Assembly Hall is different from the way the dressing facilities were designed. The Hoosiers originally were to dress in the south locker room but after one exhibition game switched to the northern location.

During an exhibition game against the Australian national team, the Hoosiers and Aussies crossed paths en route to their benches.

"That didn't happen in the first scheduled game in the building against Ball State," Crabb said. "He didn't want the teams crossing, so he took what had been designed to be the visitors' locker room. The visitors got the southern location, which became the IU women's locker room in the late 1990s."

Visitors now dress in a room on the west side of the hall.

Find Your Own Dance Floor

While the Hoosiers long have been known for their defensive prowess, they probably don't play zone defense as well as the IU cheerleaders.

After Purdue beat Indiana 96-94 on a last-second shot in 1996, the Boilermaker players took turns dancing on the Indiana logo in the middle of the Assembly Hall court.

Barring an unsightly melee, that will never happen again.

"After the game the cheerleaders make an automatic beeline to the center of the floor to protect the 'I.'" Crabb said. "That dates from Chad Austin's shot and Purdue dancing on the 'I.' That was the last dance on the 'I.'"

Everything but The Lone Ranger

The *William Tell* overture, played by the IU band as cheerleaders race around the court carrying a myriad of flags, has become one of Assembly Hall's richest traditions. The demonstration, often performed during critical timeouts late in close games, first was suggested during a trip home from a game at Ohio State.

"The *William Tell* probably started about 1979 or '80," Crabb said. "At the time I was advising the cheerleading program and we were coming back from Ohio State, talking about what we could do during timeouts that might create a tradition."

Ohio State has one of the landmark traditions among Big Ten schools. For years the OSU band has played "Hang On Sloopy" during timeouts, which has been a great generator of enthusiasm among the Buckeyes' fans.

"We kind of came up with the *William Tell* and the 10 of us in the van started talking about how the cheerleaders and poms could sort of circle around with flags and create some kind of celebration," Crabb continued. "That has become a factor for the third timeout in the second half of every game."

Crabb said when Indiana and Kentucky play on neutral courts, the Hoosier contingent always campaigns to occupy the floor during the third timeout of the second half.

"We always lobby, and the Kentucky cheerleaders agree, that the third timeout will be Indiana's and it will include the *William Tell.* So you get what Billy Packer has called the greatest college timeout in the country," Crabb said.

Like Tell, Ref was a Straight Shooter

The *William Tell* overture didn't always spark the Indiana players. Once it set a fire under Big Ten official Jim Bain, and subsequently under IU coach Bob Knight.

"This was the '82 season. Here we were sitting there with Indiana and Purdue and the great rivalry that it is," Crabb recalled. "The *William Tell* got started late. There was just a mixup in signals so the band starts playing late. The cheerleaders are out there with the flags and the horn blows.

"Jim Bain is officiating and a second horn blows. They're still out there doing the *William Tell*, so Jim blows his whistle and it falls from his mouth. He walks over to the bench and leans down to the scorekeeper and says, 'I have a technical foul against the Indiana cheerleaders for delay of game.'"

IU's public address announcer said he announced to the crowd that Indiana had been assessed a technical.

"Well, Coach Knight was six feet away and down on his haunches in the huddle. He kind of looked up and walked over and said, 'What did you say?' Boomer repeated what he had told me and that's when Knight went right across the floor and pulled all the cheerleaders together. He's saying, 'We love your support, but get off the floor.'"

On at least one other occasion the Hall of Fame coach chastised the cheerleaders for a chant that became a ritual prior to Steve Alford's free throws. The students would mimic Alford's reaching for his socks, then his shorts and then his three dribbles before shooting.

The chant was "Socks. Shorts. One. Two. Three."

"He missed two free throws one time and, unfortunately, it was seen as the cheerleaders' fault," Crabb said.

Long May They Fly

Former Virginia Commonwealth coach Mike Pollio brought his squad into Assembly Hall for a game-day walk-through in 1988, took a glance at the ceiling and said,

"They're big on banners, here, aren't they?"

One of the great sights in college basketball is the five large red banners hanging at the south end of Assembly Hall, complementing a row of banners at the north end that recognizes other significant conference and national accomplishments. The building's ventilation system moves just enough air that the banners sway gently in the breeze.

The banners were not a part of the building's original décor and first were installed in the mid-1970s.

"The banners are in their second location. Originally, they were suspended from the light window in the angled walls at either end of the building," Crabb said. "In 1995, when we did the floor renovation, we moved the banners to a location farther back."

Multiple sets of banners, which measure seven and a half feet by 15, have flown above the Assembly Hall court. They were replaced after Indiana won NCAA championships in 1981 and '87, and the north-end banners were reworked in 2001.

"There is no established criteria for the banners that are displayed. They commemorate championships," Crabb said. "[Former athletic director] Clarence Doninger wanted to see the Big Ten championship teams recognized, and two banners are dedicated to that."

One banner at the north end now marks conference championships by the IU women, who won the Big Ten in 1983 and captured the 2002 Big Ten Tournament. An extra banner was made after the 1987 NCAA championship, and it is displayed at the Indiana State Museum.

Hoosiers Played in Olympics

An Olympic banner hangs on the east side of Assembly Hall, a tribute to Hoosiers who have played for the U.S. team in the Olympic Games. Those include Bob Knight, who coached the Americans to the gold medal in the 1984 games, and Steve Alford, who was a starting guard for the U.S. during their unbeaten run to the title in Los Angeles. That team is considered one of the best ever assembled, with Michael Jordan and Patrick Ewing among the players.

Indiana center Walt Bellamy played for the gold medal-winning team in the 1960 Olympics at Rome, a team that some contend was as strong as Knight's 1984 team. The lineup included Oscar Robertson, Jerry West and Jerry Lucas.

Former Hoosier Uwe Blab played on Germany's Olympic team in 1984 and '92. Quinn Buckner and Scott May were on the 1976 U.S. team in Montreal and Isiah Thomas was on the 1980 U.S. team, which didn't get to play in the Moscow games because of a boycott by the Americans.

Knight also coached the Americans in the 1979 Pan American Games, and his players included IU's Ray Tolbert, Mike Woodson and Thomas. Keith Smart and Dean Garrett were on the '87 Pan Am team, and Damon Bailey and Todd Lindeman played for the Americans in 1999.

A Chip of Hoosier Hysteria

Hundreds of Indiana fans have small pieces of the original Assembly Hall floor in their homes or offices, the result of a promotion when the floor was replaced in 1995. The project grossed more than $2 million, and pieces are still available for sale.

The athletics department kept the two foul lanes and the center of the state map that decorated the center of the court. One of the foul lanes was installed in the IU Varsity Shop in Carmichael Center. The old foul lane represents the floor in the souvenir shop.

"It fit perfectly," Crabb said.

An Indianapolis sporting goods company offered to purchase the "I" in the center of the court, but the university declined. "We were considering the possible use in future buildings," Crabb said.

The Nearest Thing to Mountain Climbing

A sports writer covering Penn State walked into Assembly Hall for the first time in 1993. With his mouth dropping open in amazement, he called his office and said, "This place is absolutely daunting."

He was looking up from floor level. Those who sit in the top row of the balcony find it even more daunting. Truly, Assembly Hall is unlike any other college arena—and those in the bad seats don't consider that a virtue.

The 17,000-seat arena opened in 1971, and the Hoosiers promptly proved it a tough place to play by winning 58 of their first 60 games there. Nonetheless, Assembly Hall is so unique that its critics may outnumber its supporters.

The steep incline of the seating areas may be unprecedented among current basketball houses.

"When it was designed in 1955 it didn't have the modern construction technology we enjoy today for clear-span," Crabb said. "They got as wide apart as they could without involving pillars, and what that meant is that the angle of the seats is very, very steep. It almost makes it a mountain climber's delight."

University maintenance men check the roof daily during the winter to make sure freezing and thawing haven't caused problems.

"The roof itself is about two million pounds resting on 56 cables. It's one of the very few roofs that was constructed in this fashion," Crabb said. "Most of them use what you call a tension ring—such as Madison Square Garden or even Mackey Arena—where the circle and weight comes to one center point and is dispersed on the outside of the columns."

There have been discussions about remodeling the Hall, but no renovation or construction is planned.

"When Dr. [Thomas] Ehrlich was president, there was a review about whether Assembly Hall could be reconfigured for expansion with modern arena amenities, or should we simply design a new building. The criteria was looking at 20,000 to 25,000 seats," Crabb said. "There were questions about whether it could fit in the current footprint. Would we need to look at a new roof?"

University officials insist that Assembly Hall is safe. The fact that students holding balcony tickets often stay home and watch games on television has to do only with the balcony's distance from the floor.

Nonetheless, former Michigan State sports information director Fred Stabley wasn't convinced.

"He used to vow he would never come into the building," Crabb said.

Oh, My!...Dick Enberg

Before Dick Enberg became a national figure as a sportscaster, he was the radio voice of the Hoosiers. While doing IU games in the late 1950s and early '60s Enberg became known for his term, "Here come the red shirts," which he frequently uttered during an Indiana fast break.

Paul Schnepf, a graduate of Indianapolis Manual and an IU student manager, recalled the excitement when Enberg asked him to help with a telecast of the Manual-Southport basketball game. At the time, Manual had Tom and Dick Van Arsdale, who would become stars at IU.

"They were going to televise the game on WTTV and I jumped at the opportunity," Schnepf said. "Then the day of the game I got word from Enberg that I wouldn't be able to go because they didn't have enough chairs. There was one for him and one for the engineer. My claim to fame never happened."

Chapter 5

Vintage Hoosiers

Nose to the Grindstone

W.E. Keisker, a junior manager, compiled a notebook concerning the 1922-'23 IU team in which expectations of the Hoosiers were outlined.

Team rules under coach Leslie Mann included:

No eating between meals.

No eating candy.

No drinking of Coca-Cola or any soft drinks.

No smoking or use of tobacco in any form.

No drinking of coffee.

Be in bed by 10:30 p.m.

Guarding the Tooth Fairy

A newspaper story written by Stewart Gorrell faulted the Hoosiers for several things after a Dec. 7, 1923, game against the

Indiana Dental College. The writer said Indiana's defense was its weakest area in a 28-12 victory over the Dentals.

Indiana Dental didn't score a point in the second half.

The writer also seemed critical of IU's tendency to foul, noting that the Hoosiers averaged one foul per person.

Indiana's defense apparently was better in its second game of the season as Franklin College, boasting famous freshman Fuzzy Vandivier, made only one of 38 shots in a 38-18 loss to the Hoosiers.

IU suffered its own offensive indignation in its Big Ten opener against Wisconsin, which the Hoosiers lost 17-10 while making only three field goals.

Scoring from All Ranges

A box score from Indiana's 31-26 win over Purdue on Jan. 31, 1923, bore little resemblance to box scores published by today's newspapers. It broke down not only the number of shots and attempts but also the number taken from "long" range, "medium" range and "short" range.

Despite the victory over the Boilermakers at West Lafayette's Memorial Gymnasium, Indiana made only seven of 39 attempts. Michael Nyikos was only one of 13 from the field for IU and teammates Eugene Thomas and Paul Parker combined to hit five of 20. Purdue's all-conference center, Blair Guillion, made only two of 25 shots for Piggy Lambert's team.

Even with the victory, Indiana fell behind 31-6 in the all-time series, which began in 1901 and saw Purdue win the first eight meetings. Regardless of the lopsided nature of the series, the IU-Purdue rivalry commanded heavy statewide attention. Newspapers covering the game included *The Indianapolis News, Anderson Herald, Richmond Palladium, Chicago News, Elkhart Truth, South Bend News-Times, Logansport Press, Crawfordsville Review, Columbus Ledger, The Indianapolis Star, Kokomo Dispatch, The Indianapolis Times* and *Vincennes Commercial.*

All Funds Accounted For, Sir

Indiana finished the 1922-23 conference season with a 5-7 record as Iowa and Wisconsin tied for the title at 11-1. According to the records of Keisker, the season's road games left IU with a deficit of $1,506.88.

The team was allowed $600 for travel but spent $274.17 to go to Illinois, $70.50 to play at Purdue, $827.62 for a road trip that covered Northwestern and Iowa and $934.59 for a two-game swing through Wisconsin and Minnesota.

In a further breakdown, the trip to Illinois resulted in $78.35 being spent for meals, $20 for hotel rooms, $33.60 for Pullman railroad transportation, $3.50 for taxis, $3 for bandages and $3 for street car fares. Another $6 in entertainment is unexplained.

A Step Toward the Future

Indiana shared its first Big Ten championship in 1925-26, splitting the title with Purdue, Michigan and Iowa. IU had to win its last four games over Minnesota, Illinois, Northwestern and Wisconsin to pull off the feat in Everett Dean's second season as coach.

Dean had coached Indiana to a second-place finish in his first year, leaving student manager George Talbot to write in his memoirs a prophetic prediction: "It speaks well for Indiana for a great future in the great winter sport."

The 1925-26 team had a top-heavy schedule that forced the "Deanmen" to play all of the Big Ten's outstanding teams. The following year the problem was resolved with the advent of a "round robin" schedule.

Although basketball practice now begins in mid-October, with individual workouts before that, the IU team didn't really get started until the last week of November in 1925. The reason revolved around seven football players and one cross-country runner not reporting until their fall seasons were completed.

Although many Indiana fans may not have appreciated the rivalry at the time, one of IU's biggest victories that year was a 34-23 victory over Kentucky.

The Big Ten's leading scorer in 1925-'26 was Indiana's Art Beckner, who with 108 points edged Purdue's George Spradling by one point for the season lead.

During the campaign Beckner made 12 of 77 "long" shots, 30 of 89 "short" shots and 24 of 37 foul shots. He would go on to be a successful high school coach at Muncie Central and Richmond.

Another member of the team was Herman Byers, also an IU football player who went on to become an icon in Indiana high school football coaching circles. Byers played four sports at Indiana.

Making a Quick Adjustment

A manager's ledger written by senior James Johnson foretold an IU legend with the following paragraph:

"There is also possible talent in the sophomore candidates. Foremost among the second-year men is Branch McCracken, whose season on the football field has left him in good shape for basketball. McCracken starred for Monrovia High School and was one of the promising members of the freshman squad last year. His build fits him for the center position."

McCracken went on not only to become an outstanding player but to coach Indiana to the 1940 and 1953 NCAA championships. McCracken was such a great athlete that the first football game he saw was one in which he played.

Talk About Throwing Chairs

Long before Bob Knight became famous for moving furniture, Indiana had a real furniture man coaching its basketball team.

George Levis, shown here in 1921, resigned as coach of the
Hoosiers in 1922 to accept a position with a furniture factory.
Photo courtesy IU Archives

George Levis, who coached IU during the 1921 and '22 seasons, was among 18 Indiana coaches in the first quarter of the 20th century. The musical chairs ended when Everett Dean took over as coach for 13 seasons.

Levis left Indiana for a position with the Showers Furniture Factory and for a time was working in the factory in the morning and coaching the IU team in the afternoon.

Levis apparently was somewhat known for running what he called a "short-pass offense," which obviously never had as much success as Knight's motion offense or Branch McCracken's famous fast break. Still, Levis wrote an article for *Basketball World* explaining the fundamentals of his system.

Apparently, the short-pass style—along with any explanation about how it worked—was a victim of the ages.

Keeping Any Spies Out

Guess what? Closed practices at Indiana didn't start with Bob Knight, although the Hall of Fame coach certainly popularized the practice.

IU coach Leslie Mann locked the doors surrounding the team's practice court before the 1922-23 season opener against the Indiana Dentals. Mann, who was a World War I vet and had previously coached at Amherst, said he had decided to keep the team's new plays secret.

We're in this Together

Mann not only had rules for his players but insisted that the other Indiana students hold them accountable.

"The students can make or break a championship team by not insisting upon every member of a team conforming to the rules and regulations of the team," Mann wrote "It is for Indiana University you are doing this, and if you would have a winner you must show your honor, respect and enthusiasm for basketball."

Mann, who himself was a star basketball player at Springfield YMCA college in Massachusetts, expected his players to take an oath to follow team rules.

"The player that cheats and sneaks around and breaks training is a traitor, a man without honor or respect," he said. "He would falter in the pinch for Indiana, and therefore ought to be, and will be, dealt with accordingly."

Girls Were Off Limits

Mann got the attention of his players in early February, 1923, by announcing that they were to refrain from any more social dates until the end of the season. The Hoosiers couldn't even sneak in a quick date in the hallway.

"There will be no more dates, even between classes," he said.

The coach basically assured that by changing the Hoosiers' customary afternoon practices to night sessions. He theorized that since the games are at night the practices should be, also.

A Literal Battle at an IU Game

Halftime entertainment in the early 1920s offered a different twist from what the current IU band and dance corps provide. During one 33-20 home win game against Minnesota, a crowd of 2,700 was treated to the halftime entertainment: a boxing match between Indiana football captain Duke Haney and a member of the freshman team.

Friendship Crosses All Boundaries

William Silberstein was the first Jewish basketball player at Indiana and, to the best of his knowledge, remains the only one.

*William Silberstein—the first Jewish IU basketball player—
later endowed a basketball scholarship in the name of
former teammate and friend Vernon Huffman.
Photo courtesy IU Archives*

When he came to Bloomington as a freshman in 1934 he arrived in a world vastly different than he had known in Brooklyn, N.Y.

"I came from a very religious background. I went to a parochial school. I was brought up in a very secluded way," said Silberstein, now a retired businessman in Rye, N.Y. "At that time certain practices were acceptable on anti-Semitism. The Ku Klux Klan headquarters was in Indianapolis."

Most of the Indiana Hoosiers went to college in their own state; complicating matters more was Silberstein's adjustment to a new style of basketball.

"Back in high school in New York I was first-team New York and captain of the basketball and tennis teams," he said.

"I came to Indiana from Brooklyn, and there was a vast difference in lifestyle as well as basketball between the Midwest and the East. The Eastern style used the figure-eight configuration as opposed to the Big Ten, which was predicated on set plays."

During Silberstein's sophomore season the Hoosier basketball team made a trip to New York and Philadelphia to play two exhibition games. One of his best friends was Vernon Huffman, who was both a football and basketball All-American at IU. Due to the fact that the team returned to Bloomington during the Christmas holidays, the campus was virtually closed. Silberstein had no real place to spend the holidays, so Huffman intervened.

"Vernon Huffman was a Beta, and at that time the Betas were the most prestigious fraternity on campus," Silberstein recalled. "In those years being Jewish was sort of a no-no on acceptance at Christian fraternities.

"However, Vernon said, 'I want you to be my guest at the Beta house for the rest of the vacation.' That was unheard of. He was taking a Jewish kid into a Christian fraternity house where anti-Semitism was rampant."

IU's First Athletic Scholarships

It was a gesture Huffman's friend would never forget, and in 1984 Silberstein returned to Bloomington from New York to show his appreciation.

"I wanted to do something to remember his warmth, how he extended himself," he said.

A meeting was arranged by Tom McGlasson—who at that time worked for the IU Foundation, was an adjunct law professor at IU and a former letterman as a manager of the IU basketball team in the '60s—and included athletic director Ralph Floyd and Varsity Club director Dave Martin. I said, "I want to honor Vernon and to endow a basketball scholarship to his name," Silberstein told them.

Unbeknownst to Silberstein, Indiana at that time did not have an endowed athletic scholarship. It was then that the first fully endowed athletic scholarship at IU was established.

"The first athletic scholarship was called the William & Sylvia Silberstein Scholarship honoring Vernon Huffman," he said. "This scholarship was to be given to the player with the highest scholastic average. The Dean scholarship was to honor my former coach, Everett Dean, and given to the basketball player who evidenced the true spirit of Indiana University. The third scholarship was named to honor Tom McGlasson, who dedicated himself to IU in every respect and who is a good friend. This scholarship was to be given to that basketball player who showed the greatest progress scholastically. As a result of my first fully endowed scholarship at Indiana, many millions of dollars were raised by other donors to create scholarships in other sports. As a result of my first scholarship, Indiana raised close to $30 million."

Huffman was described by Silberstein not only as a two-sport All-American but an All-American boy.

"He would be typical of what you would think about if you were looking for a boy to idolize. He showed tremendous courage," his former teammate said.

When Silberstein won the coveted Clevenger Award, named in honor of former Indiana coach and athletic director Zora G. Clevenger, his family came from a wide area to attend a dinner at the Bloomington Country Club. At that time Huffman was facing a severe battle with cancer and remained bedridden.

"Somehow he managed to get out of his bed and come to the dinner," Silberstein said. "He was drawn. He had lost a lot of weight, but that night Vernon was able to sing like Louie Armstrong. The same tone, the same quality. Somehow he gained enough strength that night to get up and perform. He died two months later."

A recording of Huffman imitating Satchmo reportedly still exists.

The Dean of Classy Coaches

Silberstein also held fond feelings for Everett Dean, the Hoosiers' coach from 1925-'38. Dean had been the school's first All-America basketball player and led the Hoosiers to their first Big Ten championship before leaving to coach Stanford.

"He was one of the finest gentlemen you'd ever want to meet," Silberstein said. "Everett Dean was a clean-cut, good-looking man about six feet one who had a full head of sandy hair. He married the daughter of a banker in Salem. He was very articulate and never flamboyant. I never saw him jump off the bench or argue with a referee."

Silberstein said Dean put him in a game at Vanderbilt and he responded with three quick baskets.

"Coach took me out. He said, 'Look, I really don't want to run up a score here. This coach is a good friend of mine,'" the player recalled. "He had that kind of gentleman-like attitude. Very, very much a gentleman. I think everybody respected and loved him."

As was typical of Midwestern basketball, Dean coached a system unlike what most teams played in the East.

"In Eastern ball they used a figure-eight where you'd weave in and out until you finally picked off somebody and went in for a hook shot. The scores were low," Silberstein said. "The style of ball in the Midwest involved set plays. You might hold up one finger, which meant the center would be in the pivot and you'd

*Everett Dean was Indiana's first All-America selection. As a coach, he
made sure his players—the "Deanmen"—earned their keep.
Photo courtesy IU Archives*

throw the ball there and run around the right guard. It was all set plays. Both types had their strong points, but the professionals used mostly the Eastern style."

The figure-eight dated back to the New York Celtics and was perfected by coaches such as Nat Holman of City College of New York and Clair Bee of Long Island University.

"When we were kids in New York, just like Indiana kids shoot hoops on farmland, we'd climb the barbed-wire fences and spend all day weaving in and out and picking off our man," Silberstein said.

The styles eventually evolved into a more general system, partly because air travel opened doors for schools from various parts of the country to play each other.

Silberstein recalls the Hoosiers being good shooters for their time, but not tall. The center was six foot seven, considered huge for the 1930s. Until Stanford's Hank Luisetti unveiled the one-handed shot, most of the perimeter offense came via the two-handed set shot and one of Indiana's best shooters was Joe Platt, who later would become a successful coach at Kokomo High School in Indiana.

"Joe was a gentleman and a great set shooter. I tried to adjust my game so I would get more assists. I'd pass the ball a lot to Joe because he had an excellent shot," Silberstein recalled. "Vernon Huffman was very strong under the basket but not a great shooter. Then we had a good hook shooter in Kenneth Gunning. He wasn't very much on finesse, but he was very fast."

It wasn't until 1937 that a rule was changed eliminating the center jump after each basket. Since then, the ball has been given to the other team out of bounds.

Road Games Required Adjustment

Compiling victories on the road was especially difficult in the 1930s, when just getting to the other team's campus was an ordeal.

"I remember riding the Monon railroad, which was an overnight trip to Chicago. We'd travel all night, then get to Minneapolis in the morning and go right to the fieldhouse and do a little bit of shooting," Silberstein said.

"Then they'd give us lunch, which would always be the same. It would be a small filet, a piece of toast and half a stewed peach. Then they would put us to sleep in the hotel room until about six o'clock."

Suddenly, the players were awakened and rushed to the fieldhouse to play in front of a partisan crowd.

"It was like a daydream—or like a nightmare. You'd been in bed sleeping and resting and all of a sudden you were into a noisy crowd. It was nerve-wracking," Silberstein said. "I remember how disturbing it was to go from a sleeping atmosphere to this bedlam in a fieldhouse someplace off on a strange campus."

On games closer to home the team would travel in two automobiles, with only about eight players making the trip.

No Feely, No Touchy

In the days of Everett Dean's Hoosiers, basketball truly wasn't a contact sport.

"If you put a hand on anybody it was a foul. The game was much more fluid and there was no body contact whatsoever," Silberstein said. "It also was customary to take a foul shot underhanded. And hook shots, using a lot of spin, were prevalent. Today, players usually hit the basket clean."

"I don't remember anybody dunking. The game was much slower, although there were fast breaks, which we did. But the dribbling and ball handling, faking and footwork and looking in one direction and passing in another was prevalent. There was a lot of bounce passing."

Players Earned Their Keeps

Scholarships weren't given in the 1930s, but Coach Dean had methods of taking care of the athletes. Players were given odd jobs to put them through school.

"In my particular case, I sold programs. We made a nickel on each program," Silberstein said. "I'd make $60 or $70 each Saturday, which would carry me through a month or two months."

No wonder, considering the inexpensive cost of meals. Most of the Hoosiers went to the Gables restaurant after games.

"Everybody on the team would go to the fountain. It was always on the house," Silberstein continued. "They would give you a frosted, which was chocolate ice cream. Sunday was the only night the fraternities didn't serve. You'd go to the Gables. Thirty-five cents . . . Waldorf salad . . . all the Parkerhouse rolls you could eat . . . french fries . . . T-bone steak . . . Coffee . . . Thirty-five cents."

War and Its Aftermath

Harry C. Good became Indiana's coach during World War II, replacing Branch McCracken during his leave as a navy lieutenant. At Indiana Central, later renamed the University of Indianapolis, Good had coached the Greyhounds to a 190-52 record from 1928-'43. When Good came to IU, Indiana Central had discontinued basketball.

Good coached one Central team that won 30 straight games, but he caught the Hoosiers on a down cycle, and his first team went only 7-15. One of his typical players was Corydon native Ray Brandenburg, who was 4-F in the military draft. Carl Mercer had been placed in limited service by his draft board in Brazil, Indiana, but 18-year old Gene Farris carried a 1-A classification and reported for active duty on February 2 while leading the Hoosiers in scoring.

Five days later reserve forward Del Russell left for military duty and reported in Park Ridge, Illinois. Russell had been a backup quarterback on Bo McMillin's football team.

A season ticket to the Hoosiers during the war years cost $7.50 for 11 games and $1.25 for single games. In 1944-45 IU played home-and-home games against Camp Atterbury and even played host to the University of Mexico.

McCracken returned to coach the 1946-47 team after Indiana posted an 18-3 record and set a school scoring record with 1,183 points in Good's second season. Branch was concerned about how his former G.I.s would perform—especially Ward Williams and Ralph Hamilton, who had won All-Big Nine honors three years previously.

Among those returning from service was Lou Watson, a six-foot-four forward from Jeffersonville who had served as a gunner's mate and took part in the invasion of Normandy on D-Day. Watson, who would become McCracken's assistant and IU's head coach from 1966-71, had played two years of service basketball at the Navy Amphibious Training Base in Virginia.

Bob Armstrong had played collegiately at Indiana State as a V-12 trainee, and Murray Mendenhall Jr., who along with Armstrong led Fort Wayne Central to the 1943 Indiana high school championship, had played as a navy V-12 guard at Rice Institute. So did Dick Wehr, an Ohioan who was the only non-Hoosier on the team. Charley Meyer, another Jeffersonville product, had played at Camp Grant.

Hamilton, from Fort Wayne South, had enjoyed a 31-point game against Iowa before leaving for the service. In 30 games for the Atlanta Army Service Depot, he had scored nearly 1,000 points and tallied 60 against Fort Oglethorpe, 46 against Hunter Field and 39 against the professional Fort Wayne Zollners.

Williams had been commissioned as a bombardier and flew missions in Corsica during the war. But despite these harrowing experiences he said his most thrilling experience came via a fist fight during the Purdue game in 1943.

"Between teammate Johnny Logan and myself, 10 minutes after the game had started," he was quoted in a newspaper article after the war. "I got a shiner for my part in it."

After winning a freshman numeral at IU, Don Ritter was a navigator in the Army Air Force and participated in 28 bombing missions while based in Guam and Okinawa.

Entering the war Indiana had surfaced as the dominant team in what was then the Big Nine, or Western Conference. From 1938-43 IU's 49-15 record was better than any other conference school. When McCracken returned the Hoosiers were 8-12 in 1947-48 and followed with 14-8 and 17-5 campaigns. Not to be overlooked were a pair of victories over Purdue in 1947 for only the second time in IU history.

Players' Stature Increased

The 1949-50 team included a five-foot-ten, 160-pound sophomore guard from Corydon, Indiana, named Frank O'Bannon.

O'Bannon never became much of a star with the Hoosiers but went on to become governor of his state. After the Hoosiers reached the final game of the 2002 NCAA Tournament, O'Bannon returned to Bloomington to pay homage to the Hoosiers.

Teammate Bill Tosheff wisecracked about the governor's basketball ability by saying, "He was a little twerp who couldn't play."

A New Kind of Full Bladder

Legend has it that McCracken's first experience with basketball came when he stuffed a pig bladder full of hay and shot it at a barnyard barrel hoop on his Monrovia farm.

Chapter 6

Branch Unveils the Hurryin' Hoosiers

Burnt Into his Memory

The Hoosiers were playing Illinois in Huff Gymnasium, the cozy little place in Champaign where the Fighting Illini were especially difficult to beat.

"Huff Gymnasium was worth 20 points to the home team," former IU publicist Tom Miller claimed. "But I liked Huff. There wasn't a bad seat in there."

One game in the late 1940s came decades before the anti-smoking element enjoyed any power, and by the second half Huff was filled to the rafters with cigarette smoke.

During this close game, Indiana's Charley Meyer was taking the ball out of bounds in the very limited amount of area between the playing floor and the partisan crowd.

As Miller recalled, "You backed right into the crowd. The seats were right down on the floor. Well, all of a sudden, he takes a step out onto the court and the official whistles him down and gives the ball to Illinois. Somebody in the crowd had a cigarette and shoved it into his pants."

"We're Your Guests"

The 1953 national championship game between IU and Kansas had a major rhubarb that left Indiana coach Branch McCracken incensed, although the officials apparently made the proper call.

Kansas center B. H. Born, who had 26 points and 15 rebounds, was called for what appeared to be his fifth personal foul in the third quarter. However, Jayhawks coach Phog Allen vehemently protested that Born had only four personals and that the official scorer had made a mistake. Most of the reporters on press row also had Born with only four fouls.

Officials corrected the mistake, but McCracken said, "Your books show five fouls. Born should be out. We're your guests and you have no right to rob us."

A Cradle of Coaches

The little town of Monrovia, Indiana, located just southwest of Indianapolis in Morgan County, produced three of America's greatest coaches in the first half of the 20th century. Ward "Piggy" Lambert posted a record of 371-152 over 29 seasons at Purdue. Branch McCracken coached two NCAA champions and won 364 games with the Hurryin' Hoosiers.

The third famous coach from Monrovia was John Wooden, although the man who coached 10 national champions at UCLA became famous at neighboring Martinsville. In those days it wasn't uncommon for a small-town basketball star to wind up playing for the school in the county seat, often when his father accepted a better job in the larger community.

Monrovia now has 600 residents to Martinsville's 12,000, and the latter school won three Indiana high school championships between 1924-33.

According to Tom Miller, McCracken was offered the coaching job at UCLA before it went to Wooden and, in fact, recommended Wooden for the job when he wasn't interested.

"Branch told me they had talked to him and he had recommended Johnny Wooden because they were kids together at Monrovia," Miller recalled. "At that time John was over at Indiana State. Wooden went out there and the rest is history."

Years later McCracken mentioned to Miller that he probably could have had all those NCAA championships that Wooden brought to Westwood.

Miller said, "Oh, come on, Branch. You haven't done too badly. How many people have won the thing twice?"

Can't Take the Boy Out of the Country

McCracken served two tours of duty as the Indiana coach, breaking in during the 1938-39 season and leaving after the 1943 campaign to serve as a lieutenant in the U.S. Army. With the war ended, he returned to coach the Hurryin' Hoosiers in 1947 and retired after the 1965 season.

While McCracken was in the service, Indiana was coached by Harry Good, whose teams posted a 35-29 record but went only 14-22 in the Big Ten.

"He was just a good old country boy from Monrovia, and he had no desire at all to be anything else. That was his life," Tom Miller said of McCracken.

"Monrovia did pretty well in Branch's day. At that time they had a tournament in Cincinnati called the Tri-State. They had teams from Ohio, Kentucky and Indiana and played at the old Pickens Fieldhouse on the campus at UC. They divided the court there into two courts and would play two games at the same time. They had a mesh curtain between the two courts and the

Branch McCracken, a former IU star, coached the Hurryin'
Hoosiers to the 1940 and 1953 NCAA Championships.
Photo courtesy IU Archives

officials had different-tone whistles so you wouldn't get them confused."

With McCracken in the lineup, tiny Monrovia won the event.

Limiting His Showmanship

One of the most colorful figures in Big Ten history was Jim Enright, a Chicago sports writer of considerable girth who was a well-respected college referee. He and McCracken were good friends—sometimes.

"He and Mac would carry on a conversation during the entire game," Miller recalled. "One time Jim made a call, and all of a sudden, Mac stopped, turned around and sat down. I asked Jim later what he had said to get that reaction, and he said: 'Now, Mac, you've made your little show and you're fighting for your team. But you should know that your fly is open."

Sheriff Without a Gun

McCracken may have looked a bit gruff on the exterior, but the Big Sheriff had a way with parents of prospective Hoosiers.

"You put him in a family, and in 10 minutes he had the family ready to get in the car and take the kid up to Bloomington. He had a way with parents," Miller said.

The retired sports information director recalled accompanying McCracken to a speaking engagement in Aurora, Indiana, which was Miller's hometown.

"He asked to visit my folks and I said, 'Sure, they'll like that,'" Miller recalled. "My dad, to the day he died, talked about the time Branch McCracken came in. Branch was a well-known figure and successful athlete and he could sell the mamas and the papas, too. He could sit down around that kitchen table and he'd have the kid panting to go there."

Hoosiers Weren't Just Wild Things

Indiana's offense was unique under McCracken in that the Hoosiers had a devastating fast break. Branch explained that he usually thought he had the best players and that their chances were better if they put up the most shots.

"When he came here in 1939, Everett Dean was very cautious and didn't take any chances," Miller recalled. "Branch would gamble a little bit more, but, like Everett, he liked to play defense. But Dean was a great coach, and he had an even better record at Stanford after he left here."

Many Hoosiers from the 1950s believe McCracken's defensive philosophies were overlooked because of his offense.

"We played good defense and we worked the ball. We could slow down and play," Miller insisted. "Branch liked to take the quick shot and get the ball downcourt fast, but we played defense."

Added Bobby Leonard, an All-American in the 1950s, "People claim we didn't play defense, but they didn't know McCracken."

McCracken did whatever was needed to win, even assuming stall tactics on occasion. In those days there was no shot clock in college basketball.

Once against Minnesota, a team he was having trouble beating at the time, Branch slowed things down while sitting on a lead.

"There was no 10-second rule or no time clock," Miller said. "Sammy Miranda—from over in Illinois, a great ball handler—was our one-man stall. He'd take the ball out there and just dribble and dribble and dribble and dribble. We held the ball, I suppose, for seven or eight minutes and the crowd got into it. They began singing 'Let Me Call You Sweetheart,' like it was a dance."

Paul Lennon, Indiana's telecaster of that era, recalls that McCracken had an ulterior motive for the slowdown.

"There was an unspoken agreement among Big Ten coaches that nobody would play a zone. Minnesota had a pretty good ball team and they played a zone. Sammy Miranda just held the ball on his hip and the score at the time was like 6-4," Lennon said. "We're televising it and we're going nuts. There was nothing happening."

He's Your Man, Bill

Bill Garrett was one of the quietest and most beloved IU players of the early 1950s. But occasionally, the former Indiana Mr. Basketball was found to be a bit naïve.

"The team was on a train from Chicago to Minnesota listening to the Minnesota game on the radio," said Garrett's former roommate Bill Tosheff. "The announcers said the Gophers did this and the Gophers did that. Garrett had this puzzled look on his face and he said, 'Who's this man Gopher?'"

Whose Time Are We On?

Like a lot of other athletes in his era, Bill Garrett did not enjoy traveling by airplane, but on some of the longer road trips the Hoosiers went via the air.

Bill Tosheff, who had been a military pilot, took over the controls of the team's DC-3 on a trip to Manhattan, Kans. Tosheff had no qualms about becoming an impromptu stunt pilot.

"I did a little up-and-down move and McCracken about had a hemorrhage," Tosh recalled. "I looked back and Garrett had a blanket over his head."

During one rough flight, Garrett was fretting about his destiny and McCracken kidded him, saying, "Don't worry, Bill. We're not going to crash unless your time is up."

Replied a worried Garrett, "I'm just worried about when the pilot's time is up."

Bill Garrett was a quiet but lethal standout for the Hoosiers.
Photo courtesy IU Archives

Watson's Philosophy was Changing

During the McCracken-Watson eras, the Hoosiers popularized fast-break basketball, but at the end of Watson's term as head coach, Lou was wondering about the soundness of the system.

Following an 85-81 loss to Purdue in which the Boilermakers were more deliberate than the score indicated, Watson remarked, "I've always been associated with fast-break basketball. I played it and I have coached it, but my thinking has to change.

"It's going to take a while, but we're going to change because these clubs aren't going to play with us unless they think they have us outmanned. We'll start practice next fall with that in mind and work toward that goal the rest of the season."

The next season, Bob Knight took over as coach and installed a more deliberate offense, which rose to national fame as the "motion offense."

Bob Owens, sports editor of the *Bloomington Courier-Tribune* at the time, apparently concurred with Watson.

"The Purdue game wasn't lost on the bench; it was lost because of a philosophy which has dominated Indiana University basketball for 30 years," Owens wrote.

Added Watson, "If the scores are going to be low they're going to be low. Our kids think every time they step out on the court they have to score 100 points."

A Well-Tuned Ear

The Hoosiers traveled to road games in a DC-3 during the late 1960s, but in 1971 the university switched to a Fairchild F-27. Watson was among those who had become accustomed to the old plane.

"I used to be able to tell every little sound on that old DC-3," he said. "I remember one time I noticed something a little different about the engines. The pilot told me I was crazy, but the next day he called me to tell me that, sure enough, something had slipped over the manifold exhaust a little bit. That was why it sounded different."

Mismatch at Midcourt

One of the all-time memorable collisions involved the time five-foot-five Gary Ganakas, a Michigan State guard and son of head coach Gus Ganakas, "ran over" Indiana manchild George McGinnis. Ganakas was called for charging as McGinnis, ever the actor, fell backwards onto the court.

Said Ganakas, "Criminy! I couldn't knock McGinnis down if I stood back and got a running jump at him."

A Poor Time to Identify Oneself

Dave Shepherd played the 1971-72 season for the Hoosiers after winning the state's Mr. Basketball honor as a star at Carmel High School. Shepherd's older brother, Billy, also was Mr. Basketball and had a standout college career at Butler. The boys' father, Bill Shepherd, was coach at Carmel.

Dave was in the dinner line at IU and began conversing with a girl in front of him, finally asking her about her hometown.

"Indianapolis, where are you from?" she replied.

"Carmel."

"Oh," she said, seemingly disgruntled.

"What's wrong with being from Carmel?" Dave asked.

"Nothing, I guess. I'm just sick of hearing about Carmel and those Shepherds."

TV Rights Born in Bloomington

The Indiana Hoosiers have been one of the nation's most visible teams with their games frequently featured on network television as well as on state and regional networks. But the original telecasts stretched out perhaps 35 miles and were featured on a Bloomington television station that had a small tower above one of the downtown buildings. The Indiana telecasts set many precedents that would be picked up by other stations and universities.

Televised games in Bloomington began during the 1951-52 season, after the NCAA made it possible for its member schools to negotiate with media for television rights. Some of the IU games originally were shown on Channel 10 in Bloomington, but a trade with a Terre Haute station changed the site to Channel 4. That enabled WTTV-4 to build a new tower near Trafalgar, Indiana, which still stands.

"It's safe to say that we did every home game in the 1952-53 season," said Paul Lennon, a retired advertising executive who was the TV voice of the Hoosiers in the 1950s. His partner was Bob Cook, and interest rose quickly because McCracken's team would win the NCAA championship that season.

"Talk about being lucky," Lennon said. "Television was brand new and the IU team was blossoming into one of the great ones."

WTTV's early telecasts didn't go very far, at least not without a snowy screen.

"Maybe about 35 miles from Bloomington. Our transmitter was on Walnut Street across from the old Bloomington High School football field," Lennon recalled. "We were in a drug store and there was a transmitter on the roof of that building. Our telecasts probably got to Martinsville or Mitchell."

Lennon recalled giving a speech in Columbus, Indiana, about 40 miles from Bloomington, and a man in the audience approached him about the weak signal.

"He said WTTV reminded him of his wife, and I said, 'How's that?'" Lennon recalled. "And he said, 'Hard to get and once you do, it isn't very good.'"

IU Feared Crowds Would Decrease

The first obstacle to staging the telecasts was a rights fee. University officials were concerned that fans would quit buying tickets if the games were televised.

"It's only a valid fear if you don't have a good team," Lennon insists.""What it did for Indiana University, they should have paid WTTV. There were only two television stations in Indiana in 1949. One was Channel 6, WFBM, in Indianapolis, and they went on the air May 30 of that year. WTTV went on Nov. 11 of that year. "

WTTV agreed to pay IU $1 for every unfilled seat in the old fieldhouse and paid a $750 advance. The first telecast was on Dec. 6, 1951, and Indiana defeated Valparaiso 68-59.

"They sold out, and Indiana never gave a nickel of the money back," Lennon said. "We only paid $750 per game that whole year."

The next year the university asked for $2,500 a game and Lennon talked them into a compromise at $1,700. Part of the arrangement allowed IU to utilize the halftime intermission for its own television advertising.

"When you see that on TV today, that all began in Bloomington. That's where rights fees were born," Lennon said.

McCracken Like Knight in Some Ways

Paul Lennon described McCracken as a "mysterious man" who constantly was flailing away at officials in a manner later adopted by one of his successors, Bob Knight.

"He had the affection of everyone around him, including the media, but he wasn't much different than Bob Knight in other respects," the former TV announcer said. "He was profane and he was rough, and rough on the ballplayers. The ballplayers themselves were rough. Bobby Leonard was not above knocking one of his own teammates around if he didn't think he was playing up to snuff."

One Good Chip Deserves Another

The theory that sports advertising sells was proved by a small Indiana company that had trouble meeting the demand for its product after sponsoring Indiana basketball games.

The company was Chesty Foods, a maker of potato chips that was based in Terre Haute. Lennon introduced each telecast by holding up a large bag of Chestys and addressing the viewers. "I've got my ticket. Have you got yours?"

George Johnson, who had been a route salesman for another potato chip company after World War II, founded Chesty Foods. It sponsored the IU games for about eight years and also underwrote some of the children's shows seen on WTTV. *The Little Rascals* and *Popeye* offered other opportunities for Chesty to present its product into central Indiana homes.

"Chesty went bananas. They couldn't handle the stores," Lennon said, chuckling. "They ran out of potatoes in a couple of weeks and had to go to other states to buy potatoes out of other people's potato bins."

Johnson later sold Chesty Foods to another company and eventually it fell under the Borden umbrella. It wound up in the hands of another chip company, Seyfert's of Fort Wayne.

"Seyfert's has been very good to me," Lennon said. "I gave about 12 speeches to service clubs, and every time I gave a speech, all I had to do was call the warehouse in Noblesville and say that I needed 80 bags of potato chips at the Union Building in Bloomington for the Rotary Club. And, bingo, they supplied them. I think they supplied 120 bags for the Indianapolis Rotary Club and 110 for the Kiwanis Club. Phone call! . . . Zip! . . . Here they came with the potato chips."

Lennon appeared at an IU game in 2001 and joked about calling the firm and asking for 17,000 bags of chips.

"They probably would have sent them," he quipped.

Branch's Version of "Rope a Dope"

A regular training method during McCracken's days involved a rope inside the fieldhouse that players had to scale following a lengthy run around the area. For a slender athlete like Jimmy Rayl, the climb wasn't as difficult as returning to the ground.

"You'd climb hand over hand up to the top of that. You had to run around the state police station and around the stadium and then climb that damn rope. Well, I could get to the top, but then I had to slide down and I'd burn my hands," Rayl recalled.

The Splendid Splinter saw no logic in why such activities would help a shooter. If anything, he assumed calluses and burn marks would only disrupt his feel on the basketball.

"I wasn't liking it very well, so one time I ask him, 'What are we doing this for?'" Rayl said. "And he said, 'When you grab those rebounds you'll be strong and they won't be able to bat the ball out of your hands.'

"Of course, I didn't say anything to him, but I wondered to myself, 'Hell, I'm not down here to grab too many of those rebounds. I'm six-one and 145 pounds.' I don't know what he thought I was going to be doing. I thought that was what the big guys were for."

Be on Time; Better Yet, Be Early

One of McCracken's virtues was timeliness. Nobody was late unless he wanted to land in the coach's doghouse.

Rayl recalls an occasion where the team bus picked up players at the IU Fieldhouse and Walt Bellamy was late.

"He would leave you. We were to leave the fieldhouse and Walt wasn't there. We left on the team bus and saw Walter coming by a taxi or something, but Walter got to the airport on time," Rayl said.

Rayl said McCracken's demands later served him well in the business world, where he was always early for meetings while other employees might drag in.

"Branch knew about Lombardi Time before anyone ever used that term," Rayl said in comparing Branch to Green Bay legend Vince Lombardi. "If you were supposed to be there at eight, you'd better be there at a quarter to eight or you'd be in trouble."

Rayl, Tom Bolyard and a couple of other Hoosiers did get a break one time after a lopsided loss to the Gophers in Minnesota.

"We got in this cab to ride to the airport. The driver didn't know how to get there, and we were trying to give him directions, except that we didn't know where we were, either," Rayl said. "We got lost and we were about an hour or hour and a half late getting there.

"Branch was never so glad to see us. It was unbelievable. We had just gotten beat by 20 or 30 points and you'd have thought we'd have won the game when he saw us walk down there."

Coaches Know All, See All

Rayl is still trying to figure out how McCracken found out about an impromptu trip off campus, presumably a no-no with the Indiana coach.

"One thing about Branch, he always knew what you were doing," Rayl said. "I left the fraternity house one night during the middle of the week. I had to come home for something. I left at midnight and I got to Kokomo at 1:30. Actually, I remember that it was 1:28. I was back at school the next morning for my classes and I didn't tell anybody."

That afternoon Jimmy walked into practice and the coach met him as he arrived on the court.

"And he said, 'How was everything in Kokomo last night?' I just said, 'Fine,' and kept on walking. I didn't want to get into it. Somehow he knew. To this day I don't know how in the hell he knew I was there at that time of night, but he had a way of knowing everything."

The Game Was Over, but the Party Wasn't

Rayl has fond memories of playing against the late Dave DeBusscherre, a star at the University of Detroit who later played for the New York Knicks and is now a member of the Naismith Basketball Hall of Fame.

During the 1962-63 season DeBusscherre led Detroit to a victory in Bloomington, and with two or three minutes left in the game, play was halted for a free-throw situation.

"He was wanting to carry on a conversation, and he asked where the party was after the game," Rayl recalled. "We met him after the game, and Tom Bolyard brought him over to the SAE house. He drank, I'd say, about 16 cans of beer. We didn't drink, Tom and I.

"The thing about him that amazed me was he never went to the bathroom. He said his folks owned a tavern and said he'd been drinking since he was about seven years old," Rayl said.

Daily Break for the Big Man

Speaking of restrooms, virtually every day before practice Walt Bellamy would ask to be excused, and after a while the habit became disturbing to McCracken.

"Every single night we'd do our little drills before we got ready to scrimmage. It was kind of a little routine every night," Rayl said. "Of course, the floor was quite a ways from the restroom, and every night before we began to scrimmage, Walter had to go back to the restroom."

Rayl said McCracken had a habit of constantly repeating the same thing. "Branch would say, 'I'm gonna get him a bucket. I'm gonna get him a bucket. I'm gonna get him a bucket. I'm going to get a bucket out here.'"

Rayl doubts Big Walt had any purpose in leaving other than to irritate McCracken.

"It made Branch so mad," he said.

Well, Havlicek was a Good One

Rayl adored McCracken and often praises his coaching ability, but the former Indiana Mr. Basketball said the Big Sheriff wasn't much on game preparation.

Using Ohio State's great teams as an example, Rayl said the pregame talks would center around the various Buckeyes, whose names were written on a blackboard. "But Branch would get to John Havlicek and his scouting report on him was, 'He's a good one. He's a good one.'

"He would never say anything about he liked to go to his left, or he shoots over you in this area, or whatever. He'd just say, 'He's a good one,'" Jimmy recalled.

Bellamy Green at the Beginning

Walt Bellamy arrived on campus in the fall of 1957 as a largely untested big man out of New Bern, North Carolina. Freshmen weren't allowed to play with the varsity at that time, but there was a much-discussed game between the freshmen and varsity squads.

Bellamy had to go up against senior Archie Dees, twice the Big Ten's leading scorer at more than 25 points a game. Dees was the first two-time winner of the Big Ten's Most Valuable Player award.

Classmate Gary Long remembers the vintage Bellamy, saying, "He was so quick for a guy his size, but he was totally raw when he came here. I think he went 3-for-20 in the varsity-freshman game. He improved so much by his sophomore year and then he just kept improving. He could get the rebound, get it out and then be down the floor and be the one who scored the basket."

Walt Bellamy towered above his freshmen teammates in 1958.
Photo courtesy IU Archives

Jimmy Enright, Quite a Guy

One of the Big Ten's most visible figures in the 1950s and '60s was Jim Enright, a rotund Chicago sportswriter who moonlighted as a college official.

"He was my buddy, my favorite referee," said Rayl, an apparent favorite of Enright. "He was like a coach on the floor to me. He'd talk to me. Say, 'Settle down,' and stuff."

Enright later became the public address announcer at Wrigley Field, and years later, Rayl and a group of his fellow workers attended a Cubs game there. Upon entering the ballpark, Rayl handed a business card to a girl at an information booth, asking that his regards be passed along to Enright.

"We were all drinking beer, and I never gave it another thought. About the fifth inning, I was sitting in a box seat between innings and he came on the loudspeaker and said, 'Attention! Attention! Will Jim Rayl report to the press box? Jim Rayl, from Kokomo, Indiana, please report to the press box.'"

Rayl headed upstairs and found the Cubs' public address announcer thrilled to see him again.

"I saw the rest of the game with him and Lou Boudreau was sitting right beside us," Jimmy said. "I finally told him, 'I'd better go back with my buddies,' and he said, 'You're not going anywhere.' He was quite a guy, a good referee, too. The fans loved him. He would holler and carry on, tell you what you did wrong."

A Call that will Live in Infamy

Bob Leonard, whose free throw gave the Hurryin' Hoosiers the 1953 NCAA championship, believes Indiana should have won back-to-back titles. It all slipped away in 1954 when IU lost its opening game of the tournament to Notre Dame, 65-64.

It came down to a charging foul against Leonard in the waning seconds, a foul that Bob claims to this day should have been against the Fighting Irish's Dick Rosenthal. A newspaper photo seemed to indict Rosenthal, who later would become athletic director at Notre Dame.

"We got jobbed something awful against Notre Dame," former IU publicist Tom Miller believed. "It was just terrible. I just couldn't believe it."

Years later Leonard mailed the photo to Rosenthal, long after the two had become close friends, but the Notre Dame star never would publicly admit that the call was incorrect. Leonard also became close friends with Junior Stephens, another standout for the Fighting Irish.

"We win that game and we win our back-to-back national titles," Leonard said. "We had the rest of the tournament field covered."

Coach Didn't Throw Quarters Around

The area now occupied by Assembly Hall and Memorial Stadium was a wooded area when Leonard reported to Indiana in the early 1950s. Since practice didn't start until a couple months after school began, McCracken had his players running a three-mile cross-country course through those woods until practicing actually began.

"He would take the top three finishers out to eat," Leonard recalled. "We had some guys who had run track very successfully in high school on the team, but I was determined to finish in the top three and I'd run nine miles every day while the others were running three."

The race that year saw Leonard finish second and earn one of McCracken's free meals.

"One thing about Branch is he was very tight," Leonard said. "He took us to this restaurant and told everybody that the chicken was very good. Well, the other two guys ordered the chicken, but when they got to me I ordered a steak and shrimp.

"Branch said, 'What's the matter? Isn't chicken good enough for you?' The steak and shrimp was about $4.50, but the chicken was only about $2.50."

Golden Boy Image Tarnished

Jim Schooley, from Auburn, Indiana, was one of McCracken's favorite players on the 1953 NCAA champions.

"Jim wasn't a very good player, but he was a straight-A student, a model citizen. Never got into any trouble, and Branch was always bringing up Jim Schooley's name," Leonard said. "It was Jim Schooley would never go out drinking, or Jim Schooley never cuts class, or Jim Schooley never gets into trouble."

On one road trip, the team ate at a familiar restaurant, and afterwards McCracken got word that six steak knives were missing and the players were suspected of having taken them. As curious bystanders watched, Branch lined up the Hoosiers as if it was a police lineup and began searching through their luggage.

He had found nothing until he got to Leonard.

"He thought he was done searching then. He thought I was his man," Bob said. "He opened my stuff, and I can still see his face when he couldn't find any steak knives. Then he came to Jim Schooley, opened his bag and there were the six missing steak knives.

"We never again had to listen to him telling us about how Jim Schooley never would have done something."

Breaking Away from the Quarry

McCracken didn't do Leonard any favor when he got him a summer job in one of the stone quarries around Bloomington. The coach thought lifting stone all day would make him stronger and tougher.

"I worked out there in the hot sun and got so much dust on me you didn't know me at the end of the day. I thought, 'Darn him,'" Leonard recalled.

However, the ex-IU star admits he got to become friends with all of his fellow stonecutters and it was then that they took him out drinking and taught him to play poker.

"I didn't drink beer at that time, and I wasn't any good at poker for a while. But I learned and pretty soon I was taking their money," Leonard said.

The Only Big Dance is the NCAA

McCracken went behind Leonard's back once when a major university dance was scheduled one night before a critical basketball game. Leonard's longtime wife, Nancy, was counting on attending and her mother had made a special dress for the dance.

But McCracken paid her a visit and gently persuaded her not to accompany his star guard to the dance. As badly as she wanted to go, Leonard said Nancy decided they wouldn't attend.

"He was afraid I'd go out drinking and be out all night," Leonard said.

Wildcats and Hoosiers Sort of Met

One of the major discussions surrounding Indiana's great teams of 1953 and '54 was how the Hurryin' Hoosiers would have done against Kentucky, a school that was on probation and ineligible for the NCAA Tournament. The Wildcats, under fabled coach Adolph Rupp, went 25-0 in '54 and finished first in the Associated Press national poll. The Hoosiers (20-4) were ranked first by the United Press.

Indiana was led by Don Schlundt, who decided not to pursue an NBA career, Leonard, and Dick Farley. Kentucky was led by All-Americans Frank Ramsey and Cliff Hagan, and Lou Tsioropoulos, all future NBA players.

Fans in both states will argue the merits of their respective teams, but Leonard recalls that an All-Star game played after the season in Madison Square Garden was set up so the three Indiana players would be on one team and the three Kentucky stars would be on the other.

"We kicked their butts," Leonard said.

Don Schlundt, being measured by Coach McCracken,
was the first influential big man in the Big Ten.
Photo courtesy IU Archives

Dees, May Won Two Silver Basketballs

Twelve different Hoosiers have won the Big Ten's Silver Basketball Award, which has been awarded since 1946 to the conference's most valuable player by the *Chicago Tribune*. Indiana's Archie Dees (1957-58) and Scott May (1975-76) are the schools' dual winners.

Others capturing the honor were Don Schlundt in 1953; Steve Downing, '73; Kent Benson, '77; Mike Woodson, '80; Ray Tolbert, '81; Randy Wittman, '83; Steve Alford, '87; Calbert Cheaney, '93; Brian Evans, '96, and Jared Jeffries, 2002.

Indiana players won the Silver Basketball Award three straight times and four times in five years beginning in 1973.

Ignorance is the Spice of Life

Gary Long recalls a game at Oregon State during the 1958-59 season in which IU's Lee Aldridge seemingly crossed the line of good judgment in berating an official.

"Lee got to calling the referee a pimp," Long said. "It shows that I was from the farm and how naïve I was, but I didn't know what a pimp was. Every time the ref would make a bad call, Lee would call him a pimp and you could hear it all over the gym."

The official finally came over to coach McCracken and said, "If he says that one more time you're getting a tech."

"I don't think McCracken knew what it was either," Long said.

Some Poor Off-Court Judgment

Long was serving as the Hoosiers' captain during a road trip his senior season, which meant that his teammates not only followed his example on the court but, occasionally, off of it.

"When we'd go on these trips we always came in and ate dinner in the evening and then there'd be some free time in there, a couple of hours," he recalled. "Jerry Bass and I talked everyone into going and seeing this Jerry Lewis movie called *CinderFella*. Nobody seemed interested, but we finally got them all to go and it turned out to be the worst movie ever made. I was the guy making speeches before the game, and it was a miracle I ever got them to listen to me again."

Shooting Peaked as a Senior Citizen

Long played on various local basketball teams until he was about 50 years old, and his competitive fires still burned at that age, especially when the Great Indiana Shootout was staged at New Castle. Long's success there created some thoughts about whether he should have scored more as a collegian.

"Branch wanted me to be more aggressive. I was almost too nice a guy. I always did worry about what the crowd was thinking, or that I was shooting too much. I wish I had been more aggressive and cockier. Heck, I didn't find out until that Great Indiana Shootout what a good shooter I was," said Long, who was almost 50 at the time.

The Shootout was a gimmick event that drew great shooters from all over, the one obvious exception being Rick Mount.

"The only reason I got into it was this guy had set up a shooting contest between me and Billy Shepherd, the horse games," Long said. "I beat him and then the Alfords came to our home and I beat him. I thought, 'Gosh, I'm going to get in this thing.'"

Long said he made 66 out of 80 shots from the three-point and 17-foot distances and finished third the first year and second to Jerry Flake the next.

"The reason I didn't win was I couldn't make the 10-foot hook shot. Jerry Flake won both years because he could shoot those outside shots and also had the hook shot," the former Hoosier claimed.

During the third year Long worked on his hook shot, but the novelty of the contest had worn off and the event was cancelled.

"Of course they take better shots now, but when I look back on the guards of the McCracken era, I had a higher shooting percentage than any of them, including Jimmy Rayl. I never would have guessed that," Long said.

Early Memories of Knight

Long played against Bob Knight when the latter was a reserve at Ohio State, but he has no memory of the man who later became a Hall of Fame coach. But Long did dig up a game film in which IU beat Ohio State and Knight came in late in the game.

"He wasn't quick. I think one reason he turned out to be a good defensive coach was he was a terrible defensive player. He probably studied how to make himself better on defense and then figured the whole thing out, that defense is the key to everything," Long said.

How Do You Like Your Chicken?

Few visiting players have come under a larger assault from the IU fans than Bill Cacciatore, a guard at Northwestern from 1960-62 who unloaded on the Hoosiers in a game in Evanston.

"He was scoring like crazy against us. I think he had 20 some points against us at Northwestern," Long recalled.

The rematch in Bloomington saw a turnaround in Cacciatore's fortunes.

"Down home I think he got one basket and that was when [Walt] Bellamy goal-tended about two feet in front of the basket," Long said. "Everybody in the stands was calling him Chicken because Cacciatore was his last name. Even McCracken got to calling him Chicken. I was sitting there beside McCracken and I couldn't believe he was calling him Chicken, too."

A Case of Mistaken Identity

One of Indiana's trips to Illinois in the late 1950s came after a downtown Bloomington business had given the Hoosiers sporty new red blazers to wear on the road. Long was standing outside a hotel in Champaign when a man tapped him on the shoulder and asked him to carry his luggage.

"He thought I was the bellhop because the jackets were the same color. If only I'd have been thinking, I'd have done it. I could have used the money," he said.

Chapter 7:

29 Years Under Bob Knight

The Other Side of Bobby

Bob Knight seldom gave a speech that didn't criticize sports writers, including his famous remark that, "Most of us learn to write in the second grade and then go on to other things."

But while the coach had no use for most reporters, he did have a warm spot in his heart for a few. His best friend was former *Herald-Times* sports editor Bob Hammel. Few people realized that Knight held a warm spot for certain writers, even those with whom he had experienced disagreements.

One of those was Max Stultz, a longtime reporter for *The Indianapolis Star*. When Stultz came down with a serious illness, one that eventually would take his life, Knight helped pay his medical expenses.

Another writer who feuded with the coach was the late Bob Owens, who was sports editor of *The Courier-Tribune* in Bloomington when Knight was hired in 1971. Owens, who had worked at major papers in Chicago, Miami and Louisville, quickly landed on the wrong side of Knight's good graces.

*Bob Knight left high standards for his successor
after winning three NCAA titles in 29 years.
Photo courtesy IU Archives*

However, *The Courier-Tribune* ceased publishing in December of 1973, leaving Owens without a job. Knight used the contacts that he had to help Owens become sports editor of the newspaper in Lincoln, Neb.

A few years later when the Lincoln newspaper also ceased publication, Knight stepped in and assisted Owens in landing another job with *The Columbus Dispatch* in Ohio.

Knight often enjoyed friendly relationships with veteran reporters but was turned off by young sports writers, whom he often felt were know-it-alls. Longtime writers such as Dick Mittman of *The Star* or John Mutka of *The Post-Tribune* in Gary, Indiana, were respected and often called by their first names at news conferences.

Mittman once asked a harmless question about rebounding during the early stages of a news conference, and Knight, who was upset by the team's play in the game, lashed out verbally at the stunned Indianapolis writer.

About 30 minutes later later Knight sent a student manager to find Mittman and apologize. Then he asked some of the other reporters to come into the basketball offices, where he expressed his regret and offered to answer any questions that might have been eliminated by his outburst.

Sign of the Times

A sign in the Indiana basketball offices reflected Knight's personality. It read, "Everyone who visits this office brings happiness. Some by coming in. Some by going out."

One sports writer who had a checkered relationship with Knight wrote, "I'm still trying to decide if I'm coming or going."

Keep it Straight, Son

Knight was playing in the Foster Brooks Pro-Celebrity Golf Tournament in Louisville, and when he got to the 10th tee, a television sportscaster was rattling off nonsensical remarks about the coach over a public address speaker. Somewhere in his rhetoric a chair was mentioned in reference to Knight's 1985 flip across the Assembly Hall court.

The TV guy's jokes weren't very funny, especially to Knight, who walked over to the guy, put a hand on his shoulder and asked, "Do you know why a donkey doesn't go to college?"

Aware he was being set up, the TV guy replied, "I don't think I want to know."

"Because nobody likes a smartass," the coach said.

Careful who you Call a Friend

Knight always considered former Michigan State coach Jud Heathcote one of his closest friends in the Big Ten and once called Jud and remarked, "You're the only friend I have in the conference."

"I said, 'Don't jump to conclusions,'" Heathcote recalled.

Help Arrives from Gridiron

When the Hoosiers' roster became decimated because of injuries and a defection, Knight put in a call to football tight end Ross Hales for the second half of the 1993-94 season. The six-foot-seven, 260-pound senior had used all his football eligibility and had played basketball in high school.

Hales had returned from the Independence Bowl in Shreveport, La., where the Hoosiers had lost to Virginia Tech 45-20, when he was called by assistant coach Dan Dakich about joining the basketball team. At the time Indiana was without Brian Evans and Todd Leary because of injuries and had lost freshman guard Malcolm Sims via transfer.

Although 50 pounds lighter at the time, Hales had averaged 20 points and nine rebounds as a senior at Elkhart Memorial High. He played sparingly with the Hoosiers.

Knight reportedly considered asking Hales to play in 1992-93 after Pat Graham went down with a foot injury early in the season and Alan Henderson tore an anterior cruciate ligament in February. He decided against it because Hales still had a season of football remaining.

The International Hoosier

Haris Mujezinovic's arrival on campus in 1995 gave the Hoosiers an international flavor and also gave them a closer look at world tensions. Mujezinovic is a native of Sarajevo, Bosnia-Herzegovina, and spent his two seasons in Bloomington amid heavy concerns for his family at home. Haris came to Chicago and migrated to Northern Illinois University. Although Mujezinovic was a good student, a technicality caused him to be ineligible at NIU.

Before coming to Indiana, the six-foot-nine, 250-pound center played at Joliet (Ill.) Junior College. Despite his massive frame, Haris had been a soccer player in Bosnia.

At one low point in his life Haris considered giving up basketball, but his mother, Hafiza, talked him into playing. He realized there was nothing he could do to improve the situation in his homeland.

No Fashion Statement

The two best teams in the Big Ten in the early '90s reflected the different philosophies of their coaches. Michigan's Steve Fisher generally was seen as a "players' coach" who was willing to make concessions to modern ideas. Indiana's Bob Knight stuck with old-fashioned ideals and was one of coaching's standup disciplinarians.

Fisher coached a group of freshmen known as the Fab Five, which consisted of Chris Webber, Jalen Rose, Juwon Howard, Jimmy King and Ray Jackson. That group reached the Final Four in 1992 and '93 and was accompanied there by Indiana in '92.

The trademark of those Michigan teams was their long trunks, at that time extending to the knees and well ahead of the times. The Hoosiers wore trunks only slightly longer than those that had been worn by most teams for almost a century.

The trendy trunks became a recruiting tool for the Wolverines, but Indiana's Greg Graham may have said it best with the remark, "Basketball is not a game of fashion."

Once a Knight Guy, Always ...

Disciples of Knight who went on to coach at other schools often learned they had been cast in the Knight mold, at least until proven otherwise.

When former IU player and assistant coach Joby Wright took the head job at Miami of Ohio, he stepped into problems that eventually would haunt him. Soft-spoken by nature, Joby ran into a controversy when some of his players thought him to be a bit tyrannical.

"When I got there, I had to keep the whole staff, and both of the guys I kept wanted to be the coach. You immediately know that's not going to work out too good," Joby said. "I had never coached anywhere else. I was the first black coach. I'm a big guy. I've got a big mouth. I've got a passion for the game, and I came in there."

Wright said Miami was called a public Ivy League school and he formed some opinions.

"I said, 'These guys are soft. They're real smart and they're real good but they've got to toughen up,'" he recalled. "My goal was to do everything I could to make that come about. Yeah, I pushed them. I had a couple of situations, but invariably, instead of being a situation that Joby Wright encountered as a coach, the Wright-Knight thing came into play."

Joby said his responsibilities as an IU assistant had been different.

"I was the guy who dealt with the parents. I was the guy who smiled a lot. I was the good cop at IU, I guess," he said.

Standing Up to Coach

Knight liked to be in control of everything surrounding the Indiana basketball program. In fact, he considered himself the "athletic director for basketball."

That led to some discussions with veteran sports information director Tom Miller during Knight's early years in Bloomington.

"We had lot of go-rounds because his ideas were quite different than mine. On occasion we were shouting at each other," Miller recalled.

"He didn't want to give *Sports Illustrated* any credentials and I said, 'We can't do that, Bob.'"

"Why can't we?" Knight would say.

"I said, 'You'll be pillared coast to coast and the university will not back you up on it,'" Miller said he replied.

"He hated [former "*Sports Illustrated* writer] Curry Kirkpatrick with a passion," Miller said. "He wanted to do things that were going to reflect on him, the program and everybody else. He couldn't understand that. But a lot of times he'd end up saying, 'You know that situation better than I do. Do it your way.'"

Miller, who retired in the 1970s, has a theory on why Knight's personality was so volatile.

"I think his childhood was strange. His mother was a teacher. His father was a railroad engineer who was gone most of the time. He was raised pretty much by his grandmother," Miller said. "She played a lot of games with him because that was one way to keep him happy, but she soon found out that if he didn't win he was impossible.

"I think he grew up thinking this was the natural order of events, that if you didn't win something was wrong with the world. By and large I think I understood him pretty well and I think I stood up to him some. If you stood up to him, you might not win, but at least he respected you."

What's in a Friendship

Bob Hammel, longtime sports editor of *The Herald-Times* in Bloomington, became Knight's best friend following the coach's move from West Point to Bloomington. But Hammel, whose extreme intelligence and love of basketball corresponded with the coach's, wasn't always on Knight's good side.

Miller recalled one occasion when Knight apparently tried to get Hammel fired, apparently over the fact that the Bloomington newspaper ran a picture of Knight grabbing the jersey of player Jim Wilson.

"He was trying to get rid of Hammel, and I said, 'Bob, you may not realize it now, but Hammel's the best friend you've got here,'" Miller recalled, "and he said, 'Well, if he'd been my friend he wouldn't have run that picture.' He couldn't quite see the other side."

Holding Call Was Missed

Greg Bartram is the answer to a trivia question about Indiana basketball.

The six-foot-five Bartram is the Penn State player whose jersey was grabbed by IU's Chris Reynolds as Bartram was breaking away for a key basket with 19 seconds to play in 1993. The Hoosiers, ranked first nationally, trailed by two points in their first visit to Penn State since the Nittany Lions joined the Big Ten.

Sam Lickliter is another answer to a trivia question. He was the official who called Bartram for pushing off on the out-of-bounds pass. Television replays showed no pushoff, but showed Reynolds tugging at Bartram's jersey as the Penn State player gained a step on him.

"I ran toward the basket. Eric [Carr] threw me the ball," Bartram recalled. "When I started running he [Reynolds] had hold of my jersey with one hand and my waist with the other. I grabbed the ball and went up for a shot and I heard the whistle blow."

The Big Ten supervisor of officials later admitted that Lickliter blew the call, but it remains a play fresh in the minds of Penn State fans. It was the Hoosiers' 10th straight win during a 13-game streak.

Remember Ivan Renko?

Renko was the product of Bob Knight's imagination, which stirred emotions among Indiana fans when the coach announced that the six-foot-eight Yugoslavian would be playing for the Hoosiers.

Knight made the proclamation on his Sunday television show, saying how pleased he was that Renko would become a Hoosier. By the time he again mentioned the recruit on his Monday radio show, everyone realized he was twisting the truth big time.

For one thing, NCAA rules forbade coaches from speaking about recruits until they had signed national letters of intent. For another, Yugoslavia had ceased to become a country some months earlier. Also, Indiana had no scholarships available at the time.

Knight, who kept a tight lid on recruiting news involving the Hoosiers, apparently was trying to determine how such news was leaking out of the university.

Renko, of course, never existed.

Talk About Politically Incorrect

Many fans of Indiana opponents have screamed about the Hoosiers getting all the breaks from officials. Of course, IU fans see it another way.

But one of the most noteworthy complaints about officiating came from Minnesota governor Arne Carlson following the Golden Gophers' 71-57 loss in Bloomington during the 1992-93 season. The Hoosiers came from 12 points down in the game.

Afterwards, the governor sent a letter to Big Ten supervisor of officials Rich Falk:

"I was saddened to watch the Minnesota-Indiana game and see the referees take a victory from Minnesota. I have never written a letter like this, I must confess. I am still outraged. It was not a question of an occasionally bad call here and there, which all basketball fans can expect. It had the earmarks of a deliberate plan to simply take the game away from Minnesota. In all the years that I have been watching basketball I can honestly say that I have never seen worse refereeing.

"Indiana was physically strong and extremely aggressive, yet they were rarely called and almost never in the second half. On the other hand, every time Minnesota applied pressure the whistle blew."

Carlson's letter carried no impact except to infuriate Indiana fans. But on the Hoosiers' next trip to Minnesota, the possibly embarrassed governor invited selected followers of the Hoosiers' travel party to his executive mansion.

One of Knight's Catch Phrases

Uwe Blab, the German redhead who was Indiana's second leading scorer in 1984-85, never was known for an ability to hold on to the basketball. To say he had the hands of a blacksmith is unfair to blacksmiths.

Bob Knight perhaps put it best after Blab and his wife had a baby, saying, "I told Mrs. Blab she'd better never let her husband hold that baby unless it's over the bed."

Century Club Has Few Members

Iowa's 13-point victory over the Hoosiers in 1987 marked the first time in 467 games that an opponent had scored at least 100 points against a Knight-coached team. Iowa's 46-19 rebounding edge was critical to the margin.

Indiana got a measure of revenge a year later with a 116-89 victory over the Hawkeyes in Bloomington. Three years later the Hoosiers got some more with a 118-71 win at Assembly Hall.

During the 1988-89 season Indiana would give up 100 points in three out of four games. In the preseason National Invitation Tournament in New York, IU was beaten by Syracuse 102-78 and North Carolina 106-92. Returning to Indianapolis for the Big Four Classic, Indiana fell to Louisville 101-79. However, the Hoosiers rebounded to win the Big Ten championship.

On three other occasions a Knight team yielded 100 points. IU fell 108-89 at Minnesota in 1990 and was beaten by the Gophers 106-56 in 1994. Michigan pinned a 112-64 loss on the Hoosiers in 1998.

A Triple-Crown Reaming

Knight had novel ways of disciplining his players, some of them bilingual. Once when one of the Hoosiers messed up in practice, Knight chewed him out, using the English language, of course. Then he ordered Hispanic graduate assistant Julio Salazar to chew him out in Spanish.

That done, halfheartedly at least, Knight asked assistant Dan Dakich to chew the player out in Polish.

Untouchable in any Sport

Antwaan Randle El set multiple school records and was one of the most evasive football players in Big Ten history, but the smallish quarterback also played with the IU basketball team in 1998-99.

"He was very good, very good," then assistant Mike Davis said. "He could shoot, but he wasn't a great shooter. He just competed so hard. What he didn't have in basketball ability he made up for with his desire. He gave guys fits in practice. They couldn't keep him from bringing the ball up the court."

Facing Up to the Coach

Ted Kitchel was one of the few Hoosiers who was able to stand up to Bob Knight.

"He was tough, as far as being able to take some of the anger that coach would have with him at times," Jim Thomas recalled. "He would shoot the ball at times when coach wanted another pass and sometimes he would do it in a very cantankerous way. Of course, coach would definitely meet any kind of an uprising of that sort and he seemed to handle it in stride."

Thomas said Knight's reaction to challenges by his players sometimes depended upon the player.

"I don't think he enjoyed it. He would take it from some people and with others he wouldn't be as tolerant. He kind of had an off-and-on relationship with Kitchel in that regard, but I didn't see him taking that off a lot of people," Thomas said.

What Goes Out Must Come Back

Many successful coaches have been doused with Gatorade, although it's doubtful anyone would have had the courage to dump the thirst quencher over Knight. Still, that doesn't mean it didn't happen.

"When I was a freshman we were playing in Lexington, Kentucky, and were about eight points behind Purdue," Thomas recalled. "In the locker room coach was really giving us the once-over about the way we were playing. He told us we were not playing with the kind of fire that we needed."

As a point of emphasis, Knight picked up a plastic Gatorade jug and threw it against the wall.

"Well, it happened to bounce and come back on him," Thomas said. "It was very hard as players to keep our composure because he was right in the middle of being very angry at us. He kept going and we were amazed by that as well. It takes a lot to be able to do that."

A Funny Man, Coach Knight

Neil Reed's name will be linked forever with the end of Bob Knight's tenure at Indiana, a result of the coach putting his hands around the guard's neck in practice. But there was another situation when Knight put his hands around Reed's head.

The coach was dissatisfied with the player's concentration in practice and struck his massive hands over Reed's face.

"Now tell me," he directed Reed. "Who are the guys on your team right now?"

Uncertain, Reed stood quietly.

"You don't know, do you?" the coach said, his point having been made.

"It marked one of the many occasions when Knight added some levity to practice, a fact many of his critics had trouble understanding. Many thought practices were nothing but screaming and criticism.

"He was very astute, especially on meticulous details. Whether you were communicating or in the right position," Jim Thomas said.

Once Knight asked some of his players to jump and touch the highest point they could reach on the backboard. "If you can jump higher than I can, then practice is over," he said.

Several players leaped high up the glass, whereupon the coach said, "I can jump higher than that. Keep practicing."

"His wit and his sense of humor always lightened up the practices," Jim Thomas said. "That was a window to him as a coach. Of course, he really demanded a lot from us, but his ability to show his humor helped us to understand what he was doing."

There Was No Doubting Thomas

Jim Thomas long will be known at IU as "The Other Thomas" because one of his teammates on the 1981 NCAA champions was Isiah Thomas, later an NBA star and coach. Both players made the All-Tournament team at the '81 Final Four.

Jim Thomas described his namesake as a young man toughened by his upbringing in one of Chicago's rougher areas.

"He understood and had experience on the street. Having older brothers, he had the toughness it took to get done what he needed to do on the floor. I think that's what gave him a lot of confidence," Jim Thomas said. "He had been through some situations that allowed him to know what he could do and couldn't do, and he had been able to raise the bar on his potential."

The Thomas boys first met while playing basketball at the HPER building on campus.

"He was very crafty with the ball. He had his own unusual way and rhythm of playing the game, and he had a lot of confidence in what he was doing," Jim said.

Guyton Wavered About Early Departure

A. J. Guyton had an outstanding freshman season for the Hoosiers and was named the nation's best freshman by Dick Vitale in 1996-97.

The six-foot-one Guyton joined Isiah Thomas as the only IU freshmen to have 400 points, 100 rebounds and 100 assists.

Standout guard A.J. Guyton thought about leaving school after his freshman year for the NBA, but eventually completed his degree.
Photo courtesy IU Archives

He also had successive 31-point games against Purdue and Michigan. His heroics against the Wolverines included 26 points in the second half, which included the game-tying and game-winning baskets.

Guyton went on to a stellar career and was an early second-round draft choice in 2000, but he later second-guessed his decision to finish his career at Indiana.

"I should have turned pro after my freshman year," he said.

"We talked about it," said Mike Davis, an IU assistant at the time who said Guyton frequently visited his home and discussed his future.

"He was a different type player than the normal player at Indiana. A. J. wanted to create his own shots, and he could. He was one of the best players in the Big Ten at doing that," Davis said. "I thought A. J. Guyton had a great career here and he played during some stressful times."

Davis called Guyton a "real nice, laid back . . . not soft, but gentle, kid.

"He had problems handling some things but he handled them. I thought it was a shame he went in the second round. With the career he had here at Indiana, no one should have gone in the second round," Davis said.

Baritone Under the Basket

Knight always wanted forward Andrae Patterson to sing the national anthem at an IU game, but the soft-spoken Texan never got around to it. Still, Patterson said if he hadn't been a basketball player he'd have liked to have been a singer.

Patterson sang baritone and tenor for a gospel and rhythm-and-blues group while in high school. The group was called Harmony in Motion and Andrae also wrote some songs.

Knight said with "proper training and instruction" Patterson might have a world-class singing voice. When first discussing the possibility of him singing the anthem, the coach said, "I'll guarantee with all the great voices we've heard sing the national anthem in here over the years, he will be as good as any."

Hands Up on Defense

A woman once called into the *Bob Knight Talk Show* on the radio and asked why every hair on Steve Alford's head was perfectly in place.

"She was wanting to know if I used hair spray or just left it short," Alford said. "Coach said, 'I don't think it's either way. He just plays defense with his hands on his head.'"

Stairway to Matrimony

When Tanya Frost, Alford's high school sweetheart in New Castle, wanted to see her boyfriend, she often had to go to the gym to find him. One day she found him there with a stepladder under one of the baskets and Steve seemingly bothered by a net that was stuck.

Tanya climbed the ladder, started tugging unsuccessfully at the net, and went up another step. Resting on the back of the rim was a box with an engagement ring.

Don't Even Bother to Ask

When Alford was in the eighth grade a scholastic advisor asked him what he wanted to do later in life. He said he wanted to be an NBA player and then a coach.

"She said she couldn't put that down, so I said, 'Leave it blank, 'cause that's what I'm going to do,'" he said.

Coaching the Globetrotters

Joby Wright's coaching career started at the Camp Atterbury Job Corps and included a variety of assignments, including head coach at Miami of Ohio and Wyoming. But his most intriguing coaching job was with the Harlem Globetrotters.

Most believe there couldn't be an easier coaching job, since the Globetrotters basically never lose and have no alumni with which to deal. Their opposition, most notably the Washington Generals, shows up expecting to lose and not especially caring.

Except, Wright admitted, "Sometimes the Washington Generals show up wanting to win."

For one season Wright took one of the touring Globetrotter teams on the road, with all games played in North America. Some of their greatest stars, most notably Meadowlark Lemon, had retired, but the Trotters still boasted tremendous skill. At one time they had been, arguably, the best team in the world.

"During the course of a Globetrotters game there is some serious basketball. What is supposed to happen is the Globetrotters are supposed to show their immense athletic and basketball skills. But, invariably, some nights those guys, the Generals, came out to play. Some nights those guys said to themselves, 'Hey, we're not going to be patsies tonight,'" Wright said.

Considering their vast traveling schedule, it is not surprising the Trotters occasionally had trouble staying focused on their various methods of entertainment. As in college, leadership helped relieve the situation.

"I would get the older players, the more experienced guys, and use them as assistants to make sure the younger guys knew what the heck they were doing," Wright said. "We had some pretty spectacular performances. I thought some nights those guys were going to jump through the ceiling—literally—because they were such great athletes. No, you didn't have Meadowlark Lemon. You didn't have Curly Neal. You didn't have those guys that people considered to be old Globetrotters, but the new guys were so athletic. And some of them were so well rounded in terms of personalities that they were true ambassadors."

Wright recalls walking into gymnasiums and hearing fans say, "Hey, those aren't the real Globetrotters."

"I would tell the guys I heard somebody say that and that they had to raise their level, and they would just perform. It would be an awesome experience just to see the impact and watch the people's faces and reactions," he said.

Wright said watching the Globetrotters repeat their routines never became old.

"No, because you were trying to get a group of guys to maximize their performance. We did those same routines every night, but what made it different was one night we would be in Madison and the next night we'd be in Seattle. Travel added a dimension that could really affect people. If you didn't have guys who were mature enough, if you didn't have guys who took care of themselves, then their performances were going to drop," said Wright.

Each Globetrotter routine depended on each player being at a certain spot at a certain time. Anything less could mess up the show.

"You're dealing with guys ages 23 to 44, so how do you keep them motivated?" Wright said. "They're well paid, but the challenge as professionals was to keep them on the money. The travel was monstrous, especially if you had to both bus and fly and go through different time zones. But to watch those guys handle that was very impressive."

That's a Straight Flush for Bob Knight

One of the more popular radio shows during Knight's years with the Hoosiers was *The Bob Knight Talk Show*, an hour-long program each Monday night featuring the IU coach and Don Fischer, the Voice of the Hoosiers.

Fans listened in not only to learn more about their favorite basketball team, but in wonderment about what Knight would do next. On many occasions Fischer was left to kill time with monologues while the coach went about his other business, such as eating, talking with his staff, taking a shower, and, on one occasion, providing special background noise from the bathroom.

Such unusual sounds seldom needed interpretation or became part of Fischer's commentary. In the case of the toilet flushing sound, Fischer asked the coach a question and got only silence as a response. Then, "Whoosh."

As was his wont during such moments, Fischer started laughing.

Another time Fischer was forced to fill time when Knight excused himself to take a shower. It turned out to be a good time for a commercial, and then the show's host carried out a monologue until Coach had toweled himself off.

Eating during the show helped Knight pass the time. One of the more memorable occasions involved the coach interrupting a question to direct his wife: "Karen, get me a knife."

On another occasion the coach began eating grapes during the questioning, which wouldn't have been so noticeable except that the sound of him spitting out the seeds was fairly obvious.

Knight preferred to use a speakerphone, which allowed him to keep his hands free to do other things. One night he was taking questions while working on a gun in his garage. When the weapon fell out of a vise, listeners heard a predictable reaction.

"Shit!" he said.

"Pardon me?" Fischer responded.

Chapter 8

The Problems of Succeeding a Legend

Times Were Tough in Alabama

Davis grew up in modest surroundings in Fayette, Ala., where his mother, Vandella, instilled a strong religious faith in her children and struggled to earn a living as a secretary at an African-American high school.

"My mother really couldn't afford to take care of us. My father passed when I was 12. He had open-heart surgery and was in Denver, Colo. I never stayed with him," Mike said.

The Davis home was so modest that Mike's older brother, Bill, stayed with his grandparents and his sister, Janice, lived with an aunt and uncle. Mike's brother, Van, who is two years older, and Mike shared a small room.

"It's still there. I go back and I can't believe that's where I stayed," Mike said. "I was really ashamed of it when I was growing up. I used to play football and basketball and baseball and I'd have coaches bring me home. I would always point to the house next door, which was my grandparents' home, and they'd drop me off there and I'd walk back to my house."

In Mike Davis's second season as IU head coach, the Hoosiers shared the
Big Ten title and reached the NCAA Tournament title game.
Photo courtesy IU Athletics

Van, who Mike claims was a better player than he was, played collegiately at Jacksonville State.

Just Another Businessman's Lunch

It was basically understood that Indiana needed to hire an African-American coach at the end of the 1996 season, but speculation centered around former IU players such as Mike Woodson, Bobby Wilkerson or Keith Smart. Most were surprised when Knight hired an Alabama assistant named Mike Davis, who wasn't well known in the Midwest.

John Treloar and Pat Knight were IU assistants, and Treloar knew Davis from their days in the Continental Basketball Association. Davis met Pat Knight while scouting an All-Star game and was visited by assistant athletic director Steve Downing before coming to Bloomington for an interview.

Downing met Davis at the airport and took him to the delicatessen at the Marsh food store on Bloomington's north side. Knight and his assistants often could be found in the no-frills dining room during lunch, and Davis sat down with the head coach.

"He had a couple of guys with him. I think one guy was from Colorado," Davis recalled. "I just kind of sat there for about an hour. I didn't say much or eat much." Feeling largely ignored, Davis said he reached the conclusion that there was no way he was going to get the job.

"I wasn't sure what he was thinking. I was really quiet. Sometimes when the conversation is slow, you don't feel real confident," he said.

Davis said he later met Knight for dinner along with assistant coach Craig Hartman.

"He kind of explained to me the whole Indiana situation. He said he wasn't sure if he wanted me to be on the road recruiting or to be the restricted coach," he continued.

Davis went home and told his wife, Tamilya, "Well, I didn't get the job."

IU is no Place for Softness

Among the more cutting remarks Davis made during his first season at the helm of the Hoosiers was that Indiana had a reputation for playing "soft" in recent years. By the time Indiana wiped out Duke and Oklahoma in the 2002 NCAA Tournament, no one was talking about a soft underbelly at IU.

However, Dane Fife backed up Davis's original feelings.

"I completely agreed. We had several players … First, they couldn't handle being yelled at, and second, they couldn't handle physical pain," Fife said.

Fife told Davis that the Hoosiers should recruit some players who also had played high school football. He said his father, Dan Fife, had prospered by that philosophy while coaching Clarkston High in Michigan.

Tom Coverdale also agreed with Davis's early assessment of the Hoosiers, "He showed us the things he was talking about during film sessions. A lot of our players took that to heart, and that's what changed this team," Coverdale said.

Davis compared some previous Indiana teams with a 12-year-old boy who was giving up his milk money daily to a 15-year-old bully on the block.

"That's the way it was for us last year. There was no toughness at all," he said shortly after being named interim coach in 2000. "I'm going to push them physically to the breaking point. I need to know who's going to play hard at Michigan State and who's going to quit at Michigan State."

Energy in a Small Package

The Littlest Hoosier stood on the sideline at Rupp Arena, his curly hair extending from the top of a red Indiana basketball uniform. His favorite team was enjoying a lighthearted moment at a public practice leading into IU's first Sweet Sixteen game in eight years, a 2002 battle the next night against No. 1 Duke.

With each reverse dunk the crowd reacted with oohs and aahs, but the Littlest Hoosier was the most impressed fan in the house. As each ball was slammed through the rim he simultaneously screamed and performed his best vertical leap. Antoine Davis, age three at the time, was becoming the most popular person in Rupp Arena; remember that those in Indiana uniforms have never been popular there.

Antoine, often called A. J., moved into the crowd as the practice continued. Soon, the Littlest Hoosier was signing autographs—a formidable task for one who hasn't learned to write. Fans shoved a paper and pen into his hands and, with great flair, the son of IU coach Mike Davis milked his popularity to an extreme. Each paper was returned with a scratch mark. Some fans asked A. J. to take the paper and get players' autographs and the Littlest Hoosier obediently headed for the floor.

When the practice ended, the coach's son joined the rest of the Hoosiers at midcourt for their traditional high five. Antoine was lifted by the players so he could swat palms with those five feet taller. This ritual became a tradition during Davis's second season as coach, and if the Hoosiers dared break the huddle before Antoine got there, his piercing squeal guaranteed they would have to huddle again.

Antoine always is the centerpiece of an Indiana practice. Assembly Hall is his playroom and the IU players, and especially the student managers, are his nannies.

As someone once said of the student managers, "Antoine thinks anyone in crimson and gray works for him."

On one occasion, Antoine and his caretaker were outside the Indiana locker room during a period reserved for private mo-

*Antoine Davis, being held by his father, made Assembly
Hall his playground after dad became head coach.
Photo courtesy IU Athletics*

ments with the coach and team. Antoine told the man with him
that they should go on in.

The wiser, older head hesitated, telling the youngster that
this probably wasn't the proper time to interrupt.

"It's okay," Antoine assured him. "You're with me."

It's a bit early to talk about recruiting the kid, but IU would
be wise to put his name in the computer. Antoine has a pretty
decent shooting percentage when lofted within a couple feet of
the basket. Dad performs this lifting duty best, but no player,
student manager or reporter is exempt from the task.

While Antoine's future classmates are dribbling cheap basketballs on gravel driveways, the Littlest Hoosier dribbles regulation college balls around a 94-foot court. If that becomes boring,
he has a tiny scooter that can speed down the court like the
Hurryin' Hoosiers in their heyday.

On a couple of occasions, A. J. unfortunately got his hands on a referee's whistle. His dad nipped that in the bud, as Barney Fife used to say.

Once, when a cute girl of similar age showed up at practice, the seemingly lovesick Antoine escorted her around the arena while tenderly holding her hand.

Basketball heroes always get the girls.

Friendship Forms in Back of Bus

Jared Jeffries was Antoine Davis's favorite player for a while, and then the coach's son switched his allegiance to Jeff Newton. But by the time Indiana had reached the 2002 Final Four the three-year-old was inseparable from Dane Fife.

"That was a little scary. It was like, 'Oh, my, Dane Fife could really put some things in his head,'" Davis said. "It was mind-blowing because they kind of clung to each other. They kept everybody on the team loose."

In the beginning Antoine sat at the front of the team bus with his father.

"Then when the players would walk through you could tell he wanted to go with him," the coach said. "Finally, he got up the nerve to go back there and I could hear him cutting up, talking loud and laughing. I would look back and he would smile and wave, like he wasn't doing a thing, so the players knew that they could have fun with him."

Antoine soon gravitated to Fife.

"At one point I thought they were brothers, which is scary in itself," assistant coach Jim Thomas commented. "They really developed a unique bond, especially during our run. It was comical at times and very heartfelt at others."

Players and coaches agreed that the coach's son helped keep the Hoosiers loose.

"I would hear him back there mimicking what the guys were saying. They'd be cracking up in the back of the bus. He was a great antidote. He really helped us out during those tense moments," Thomas said.

Added Davis, "It was great for the team and it was great for me. It loosened me up a lot and then the players got a chance to see me with him. I don't care who you are, if you're with your kids, you're different. They saw me in a different light and it really relaxed me with them."

Haston Found His Niche

Kirk Haston's meal ticket to an NBA contract was the three-point shot, but the six-foot-nine IU graduate didn't even make a three-pointer until his third year with the Hoosiers.

As a freshman and sophomore, Haston attempted only two shots from beyond the arc, but in his last year with the Hoosiers he made 26 of 69 and may have been the best clutch outside shooter in the Big Ten. The outside shot, coupled with his already present hook shot, was a major factor in the Tennessee native becoming the 16th pick in the NBA's 2001 selection.

Would Haston have been equally prolific from 20 feet had Bob Knight continued as coach? Former teammate Dane Fife is among those who believe that he would have been.

"I think Coach Knight would have recognized all the abilities that Kirk had," Fife insisted.

Haston first surfaced as an outside threat during a Midnight Madness shootout, the type of thing Knight never would have permitted. Under the Hall of Fame coach, Indiana's opening midnight practices were merely public practices with no fanfare. When Davis took over, the Hoosiers could officially call it Midnight Madness and bring in the various dunking contests and gimmicks that other colleges employed. In fact, Davis took the madness to a new level by allowing the IU women's team to participate.

The first time both teams conducted three-point shooting contests, Haston won for the men. Then, in a stunning revela-

*Kirk Haston became one of the Big Ten's best players after unveiling
previously unrecognized accuracy from beyond the three-point arc.
Photo courtesy IU Athletics*

tion, Haston competed against women's champion Heather Cassady and lost. Cassady, a five-foot-seven point guard who hit six successive three-pointers in capturing the women's competition, then made 17 threes in one minute while Haston drilled only 12.

Possibly embarrassed, Haston pulled his jersey over his head.

A. J. (Always Jabbering) Moye

A.J. Moye came to the Bloomington campus with an abundance of energy and conversation. Reporters quickly learned that Moye was a good source of quotes, believable or not.

"A. J. is the type of person who will say anything on his mind. Whether he thinks it's crazy or not he'll still say it," teammate Tom Coverdale said. "I think you have to have a guy like that in the locker room who kind of loosens up the atmosphere."

As a sophomore, Moye described himself to one writer as being a "young leader" on the Hoosiers, which caused Jared Jeffries to break into laughter.

But Kyle Hornsby could see through Moye's confident remark.

"We're so focused that we don't think to celebrate, but A. J. comes in and all of a sudden you see energy coming out of him. In that respect he is a young leader," Hornsby said.

Moye's popularity peaked during his sophomore year when IU fans at the regional in Lexington, Ky., began chanting: "A. J. Moye! A. J. Moye!"

"I look at his energy and it blows my mind, especially when they start chanting his name," Davis said. "He's got my little boy chanting his name."

Said Moye, "It could cause you on occasion to lose focus. If you've got 20,000 fans chanting your name you feel like you can do no wrong sometimes."

A. J. says he's the butt of a lot of jokes, but he doesn't seem to mind.

"I'm a lovable guy. I get along good with people. It's just how I am. You have to have carefree personalities."

Moye has multiple tattoos on his body. The most telltale one says, "It's not easy being me."

Davis Knew What He Was Getting

Jeff Newton was a childhood friend of Moye's in Atlanta, but there is a world of difference in their personalities. While Moye is effervescent, Newton is as laid back as a fallen log. That caused some concern for former teammate Dane Fife when he first met Jeff.

"It was Midnight Madness my freshman year. Newt was on a recruiting visit and was over on the bleachers sleeping," Fife recalled. "I was just a freshman, but that wasn't the type of player we wanted."

Fife said he approached then assistant coach Mike Davis and questioned whether Newton had enough fire within himself to play at Indiana. Davis assured him that he did, and the first time the tall Georgian worked out, Dane took another approach.

"He was unbelievable. Maybe he was having the game of his life, but he was sweet, and that changed my mind right there," Fife said. "I said, 'This guy is unbelievable,' and Coach Davis was like, 'I told you he was.'"

"I Might As Well Block It"

For years, Indiana fans will talk about A. J. Moye's block of Carlos Boozer's shot during the Hoosiers' victory over No. 1 Duke in the 2002 South Regional.

The often wordy Moye, who stands six foot three to Boozer's six foot nine, described it this way:

"I thought he was going to try to go up and dunk it and I said, 'I'm going to jump as high as I can and probably foul him.'

And then I realized I was up higher than him so I thought, 'I might as well block it.'"

Astonished at the explanation, Davis replied, "You thought of all that in a split second?"

It's Different on the Bench

Davis was known as an outstanding defensive player at Alabama whose intensity was a factor in his being selected by the Milwaukee Bucks in the second round. But the same intensity doesn't always serve him well as a coach.

"The thing I wasn't prepared for was the media part of it and being able to control my emotions," he said. "As a player I played as hard as anyone, and as a coach I try to coach the same way. But you can't coach that way; you have to coach a basketball team and not get caught up in everything."

Who Would Have Guessed?

One of the low points of the 2001-02 season for Davis came with successive losses to Miami and Kentucky. It was the weekend before Christmas, and the IU coach already was looking ahead to the following season when an outstanding freshman class would arrive. That 66-52 loss to Kentucky left the Hoosiers with a 6-4 record and only two of the 10 games had been played in Assembly Hall.

Davis summed up his feelings with the remark, "We're not going to win a national championship this year."

Of course, that turned out to be prophetic, but Indiana stunned everyone by coming within a single game of winning the championship.

Calling Signals was Tough

Davis's onetime problem with stuttering has been overcome, but the memory remains.

"I'd rather do anything than give a speech in front of people. I'd rather run 100 miles," he said. "Everyone in my family speaks well. Everyone in my family can sing. I can't sing a lick."

His onetime speech impediment may have kept him from being a football star as well as a basketball standout.

He started out as a football quarterback who even had trouble saying, "Hut! Hut! Hut!"

"I wanted to be this big-time quarterback, not realizing that you had to call the plays out," he said. "I moved to running back, because at running back you don't have to say a word."

Davis said he quit football in the eighth grade, partly because of his speech difficulties.

"In football they like for you to scream and holler. I didn't like that, so I didn't play anymore," he said.

Never On Sunday

NCAA rules prohibit athletic teams from practicing every day of the week, and many coaches alternate the day off to best fit that week's schedule. But IU's Davis always takes Sunday off.

"We never practice on Sundays. Ever." he said. "I think that's the day for guys to go to church if they want to."

Davis recalled as a player there were Sundays when parents came to visit and had to say goodbye when their sons left for practice. Not only does he not expect his players to come in on Sunday, but he doesn't expect his assistant coaches to do so, either.

"If they come in, it's on them. If my guys come in and shoot, it's on them," he said.

Jared Almost a Dookie

Former Hoosier Jared Jeffries played against Duke only once in his college career, but his IU team got the best of the other school he seriously considered attending. IU beat the Blue Devils 74-73 in the 2002 Sweet Sixteen.

Jeffries, Indiana's 2000 Mr. Basketball at Bloomington North, said he was leaning toward Duke after his official visit there. But Jeffries was close to then IU assistant Mike Davis and wanted his parents to have a chance to watch him play.

"We knew it was a stretch trying to recruit him," Duke coach Mike Krzyzewski said. "When you drive to his home you pass Assembly Hall. I thought it was worth a shot and it was."

That's Our Grandson

Judy Fife took her normal seat about six rows above the floor on the west side of Assembly Hall, her eyes piercing the air toward the court where her third grandson, Dane, was practicing with the Hoosiers. It was a regimen she would follow virtually every practice during Dane's four-year career at Indiana.

A couple of seats away, usually a row higher, sat her 80-year-old husband, Duyane.

Judy, 76 herself at the time, intently watched the court while Duyane chatted freely with the few other spectators in the Hall. Grandpa Fife, as he came to be known among sports writers, always was aware of what was going on in practice but didn't let that stop him from talking about basketball, Social Security checks or whatever else caught the interest of an 80-year-old man.

Meanwhile, Judy Fife's stare never wavered from Dane and his teammates.

One reporter decided the Fifes, who had rented an apartment in Bloomington during Dane's term with the Hoosiers, would make an interesting story. He first approached Dane about the idea.

*Jared Jeffries was a homegrown Hoosier, but after two
seasons at Indiana he decided to take his versatility to the NBA.
Photo courtesy IU Athletics*

"Just make sure if you talk to Grandpa, you also talk to Grandma," Dane requested.

As always, Duyane Fife enjoyed every conversation and spun the tale of how he and his wife had also watched most of the practices involving their other grandsons, Dugan and Jeremy. Dugan was a guard at Michigan and Jeremy played at Grand Valley State.

Moving from Grandpa to Grandma, the reporter was told to wait until practice was over. Even after seeing hundreds of practices Judy didn't want to miss a single moment of the latest one.

Over the four years the Fifes were present at every IU home game, taking their 11th-row seats in the middle of the east stands, and made numerous road trips.

With their youngest grandson completing his eligibility, the Fifes resettled in Carrier Mills, a town of about 2,000 in Southern Illinois. The couple formerly lived in Clarkston, Mich., where their son, Dan, coaches the high school basketball team and where Dane and his brothers played. From that point they drove the 50 miles to Ann Arbor for Dugan's games and the two hours to Allendale, Mich., for Grand Valley State games.

Makeup Call in Lexington

As a player at Alabama, Mike Davis got more than a little tired of Kentucky's basketball team, which has dominated the Crimson Tide and the rest of the Southeastern Conference for decades. So Davis, displaying his typical vein of honesty, struck a nerve in the Bluegrass when he ripped the Wildcats before Indiana's 2001 date with Kentucky in Indianapolis.

"I hate Kentucky—with a passion," he said. "That was the measuring stick in the SEC—Kentucky. If you can beat them, that would say a lot about your program. In the SEC, Kentucky was always the team."

Naturally, Davis's remarks were posted in the Kentucky locker room before the UK-IU meeting, and when the Hoosiers wound up playing in the South Regional at Rupp Arena later in the season the IU coach had some frayed feelings to soothe.

"I love Kentucky," Davis said repeatedly during press conferences at the tournament site. "I apologize if I ever said anything to offend Kentucky…I just want to make it clear that I do love Kentucky."

Were Hoosiers Satisfied with Runner-Up?

Until their 64-52 loss to Maryland in 2002 the Hoosiers had never lost a NCAA championship game in five appearances. In retrospect, their coach wonders if they weren't content just to have made it that far.

"I could be totally wrong, but I thought we were happy just to be in the championship. Before the game it was a different team. Normally before a game we're loose, but not that loose. Normally there's a nervousness about us, but I saw a team that was loosey-goosey," Davis said.

The game was one of the sloppiest in championship game history. Each team committed 16 turnovers, and Maryland's star point guard, Juan Dixon, had seven. The Hoosiers shot only 35 percent and were two of seven at the foul line.

"We had to make it sloppy because Maryland was a better team than Duke," Davis said. "Their inside guys were athletic, strong. We just didn't make plays with our inside people. If they do anything, if they just come out and play …"

Coverdale's Trip Rescheduled

One of the hardest things Davis did in his first two years as coach was to dismiss Tom Coverdale from the Big Ten team selected to tour Europe in the summer of 2001. Davis was coach of the team, which enabled him to pick two Hoosiers for the squad. Every other conference team had one representative.

Tom Coverdale's outside shooting and unlikely drives down the
foul line were no more important than his grit on the court.
Photo courtesy IU Athletics

But when the players gathered in Bloomington in preparation for the trip, the IU coach scheduled a morning practice that Coverdale missed. The former Mr. Basketball from Noblesville reportedly overslept, and Davis felt he had no choice but to leave Coverdale at home while teammate Kyle Hornsby went along.

"It was tough. It was really tough, but it was something I had to do," the coach said. "I knew people wouldn't like it. They want kids to act right and do right, but they don't want you to discipline them."

Davis said Coverdale understood the situation and held no grudge.

"I knew he would be embarrassed by it, but at the same time it helped him mature. He was a great player here, just an unbelievable player."

There was one consolation for Davis, and eventually for Coverdale. He had another year of eligibility, and Davis named him to be IU's representative during the 2002 trip overseas.

"There was no doubt who was going. No doubt," Davis insisted. "I knew last year who was going to go. I think Tom really appreciated the opportunity."

Sometimes Words Just Slip Out

Profanity has been a rare commodity during Indiana practices since Davis was hired. It takes a special situation for the religious coach to say a bad word.

"I do it, but I don't do it in regular conversation, and I think that's the difference," he said. "Sometimes I say, 'I'm not going to say a bad word,' but it just comes on so quickly. I feel real badly afterwards."

Run for Your Life

A centerpiece of every Indiana practice is a series of wind sprints, which are more prevalent before the season but still existent in early March.

"I like for guys to be in condition. I like for them to have that feeling. When you sprint you get tired quickly. When you jog it hurts, but when you sprint it takes a lot out of you. I want them to know that feeling," he said.

Bob Knight depended more on unrelenting basketball scrimmages and drills to get his players in shape.

"On offense we've struggled sometimes, and rebounding we've struggled sometimes. But from a conditioning standpoint we've been able to play defense the way I wanted it," Davis said.

"IU Not Great, but Never Average"

Kelvin Sampson, whose Oklahoma team was beaten by Indiana 75-63 in the 2002 national semifinals, said the Hoosiers won five NCAA Tournament games by being the best on the court on that particular night.

"The best teams don't always win, but the teams that play the best," Sampson said several months after the tournament. "They outplayed Duke. They outplayed us. It's not a popularity contest where you check the box and mark down which is the best team. For 40 minutes on the day you play you've got to play better than them, and that's what Indiana did."

Sampson said he was happy for the Hoosiers because "I like tough, gritty teams and they were tough and gritty."

The Oklahoma coach said IU's guards that season, Tom Coverdale and Dane Fife, were never going to have great highs. But, he said, "They were never going to have great lows, either. They're steady and I think Indiana's team was like that."

His Reputation Preceded Him

Mike Davis arrived at Indiana with the reputation of being an outstanding recruiter, but Davis said he had virtually no experience recruiting at that time.

"My first year recruiting was at Indiana. I had no idea how I was doing, to be honest. I didn't know Corey Maggette from any other player," he said.

Maggette, who wound up at Duke, was a standout high school player when Davis arrived at Indiana. The class also included Richard Jefferson (Arizona) and Quinton Richardson (DePaul).

Among the recruits Davis helped guide to Bloomington were Kyle Hornsby of Anacoco, La., Jeff Newton of Atlanta, and George Leach of Charlotte, N.C. In some cases, Davis said, he felt pressure over whether his recruits would make it at Indiana.

"I didn't have that feeling with Hornsby because I knew how hard he worked. That's what I was trying to find, hard workers," Davis said. "I was lucky getting the big boys. Newton was talented and Leach was talented, but I didn't know how hard they would work. But I did know they were different-type players than Indiana had had in a while. I was just hoping they'd get past the first year. Once you get past the first year you're pretty much in."

Davis said he believes none of those three would have come to Indiana had schools in their home states shown more interest. Louisiana State was undergoing a coaching change at the time, which helped Hornsby decide on the Hoosiers.

"But if Georgia or North Carolina had really pushed hard the other guys would have been tough to get," he said.

He's No Big Spender

Davis's contract at Indiana calls for him to make more than $800,000 annually, with additional incentives for other success on the court and in the classroom. But his newfound wealth hasn't resulted in much wild spending.

He did buy his wife a BMW even before the lucrative contract was signed, but extravagant spending isn't part of the Davis budget.

"I bought the car when things were really up in the air. I just figured that if she went through this with me that I could buy her a car," he said.

The Davises bought a home in Bloomington shortly after the contract was finalized, but not until the coach complained long and hard about how much money it was going to cost. Even Mike jokes about frequenting an all-you-can-eat restaurant when his expense account would allow pricey steaks.

"I love Golden Corral," he said, citing a middle-class eatery. "All the big-time coaches wouldn't dare eat in a Golden Corral. You'll see them at those fancy places, but every day I was going to Golden Corral.

"People kid me about it. They call it Mike's spot. They say, 'He's going to Golden Corral all the time.' But for $8 you can eat all you want."

Davis recalled making an eight-hour drive to appear on a radio show, a point the show's host mentioned to the audience.

"They say, 'Here's a guy making all that money and he drove up here.' I was thinking, 'Man, that's true. I could have caught a plane.' But sometimes you just forget because of old habits," he said.

Davis told of eating a meal with some other coaches.

"I was still hungry so I decided to get dessert and asked what they had," he said. "They said, 'Cheesecake and whatever,' and I asked how much the cheesecake cost. This assistant coach from Auburn says, 'I can't believe you asked how much cheesecake costs with the money you're making.'

"I always asked how much it is, because I wanted to make sure I had enough money to pay for it."

It Has to be the Shoes

Davis made suggestions upon becoming head coach that he might get rid of the peppermint-striped warmup pants and put players' names on the back of their uniforms. That may have been the players' preference, but it certainly wasn't the fans'. The new coach was swamped with requests that the status quo be maintained.

"Indiana has great tradition. If it's not going to affect us on the court, why change it, I just figured," he said. "Heck, if they want the candy-striped pants and no names, that's not going to affect the game. I just decided that they don't change things at North Carolina or Kentucky, so why should we? I'm not going to be the one who makes that move."

Bob Knight's teams wore Adidas athletic shoes for years, until the Hall of Fame coach changed to the Converse brand. When Davis took over he switched to Nike.

"Shoes are important. Kids want to wear either Nike or Adidas. The other shoes they really don't want," Davis said.

The coach said the IU players didn't like wearing Converse, adding that shoes can affect a player's choice of a college.

"It's sad, but it's true," he said.

This is No Toy, A. J.

A. J. Moye was suffering from a respiratory problem that would keep him out of the game at Michigan State in 2003 and, as a result, was dispatched to a second plane for the trip to East Lansing.

The aircraft was smaller than the normal team plane, and when the hangar door was raised, Moye got a first look at his ride to Michigan. The plane was smaller than he had expected.

"No way I'm getting in that thing," he said. "Not that Hot Wheels with wings."

IU fans insisted Davis retain the peppermint-striped
warm-ups, which the Hoosiers wore to the 2002 Final Four.
Photo courtesy IU Athletics

Motion Offense not for Everyone

Davis installed a familiar offense when he was named interim basketball coach in September of 2000, replacing Knight's popular motion offense with more of a set arrangement.

"Maybe some coaches are smarter than I am, but I came from the CBA where we used to run sets and would get the ball to people who could score. Coach Knight knew the motion in and out, but I really didn't know it. I think it takes three or four years to understand it," Davis said.

Knight once said one reason the Hoosiers didn't recruit many junior college players was because their two remaining years didn't give them enough time to learn the Indiana system.

"The thing about the motion offense is you have to be able to get in sync with the people you're playing with," said Davis's assistant and former Knight player Jim Thomas. "Each group is different. It takes time to get that process down, but it's well worth it if you're committed to it."

Thomas said learning the motion offense is difficult and it helps when players know the habits of their teammates.

"You have to continually groom it to where you know where other guys are going, and they know where you're going," he said.

Son Adds Salt to Wound

Among the lowest moments in Davis's life was the Kentucky game in Freedom Hall on December 21, 2002, where his Hoosiers not only lost but Davis lost his cool and rushed onto the court as play continued in the final seconds. Official Bert Smith assessed him two technical fouls, and Davis was suspended for one game by the Big Ten.

Davis showed great remorse during a postgame press conference and then joined his wife and two sons for the trip back to Bloomington.

"You can't believe how down I was," the coach said, "and then Antoine looked up and asked, 'Are you ever going to beat Kentucky?'"

Chapter 9

Some Especially Memorable Games

2002—IU 74, Duke 73

The 2002 Hoosiers made their first trip to the Sweet Sixteen in eight years, but the roadblock was formidable. Defending NCAA champion Duke stood in their path on March 21 in Lexington, Kentucky.

Assistant coach John Treloar helped prepare IU for the challenge by pointing out other great upsets. He showed the players a film of Buster Douglas's stunning knockout of Mike Tyson. He showed them a film of North Carolina State's upset of Houston in 1983, and he displayed a film of Villanova's nearly perfect effort in upsetting Georgetown for the '85 title.

"Nobody gave them a chance. Nobody gave us a chance," coach Mike Davis said.

One Duke administrator flagrantly ignored IU's chances during a pre-tournament meeting in which he asked what schedule his team was to follow on Saturday, the date of the Elite Eight game.

Nonetheless, Indiana stunned the Blue Devils after trailing by 17 points in the first half.

"I didn't think it was an upset," Davis said. "It's an upset when nobody thinks you're going to win, but I thought we could win if we executed. I didn't think they could handle our system that we ran on offense if we executed."

Most fans thought the Hoosiers, who were slowed by an ankle injury to Tom Coverdale, didn't match up with the Blue Devils. However, Davis saw it another way.

"I thought our matchups with Duke were good, not from a guard standpoint but from an inside standpoint," said the IU coach, believing that if the Hoosiers put defensive pressure on Duke's big men they could be stopped.

The IU coach said his team got away from its game plan early, but when the Hoosiers toughened their inside defense they began playing Duke evenly.

"Most teams in the country do not lock in defensively and play tough for 40 minutes, and I knew we would," he said.

1960—Ohio State 96, IU 95

Indiana and Ohio State were the dominant teams in the Big Ten in the early 1960s, a period in which the Buckeyes won their only NCAA crown in '60 and finished second to Cincinnati each of the next two seasons.

Indiana's visit to St. John Arena on Jan. 9, 1960, produced one of the classic battles of the series. The Hoosiers already had dropped their first two conference games to Purdue and Northwestern and would lose a one-point heartbreaker to Ohio State.

That three-game blemish was unique, because the Hurryin' Hoosiers enjoyed a 20-4 season and didn't lose another game all season. They beat the Buckeyes 99-83 in the middle of a season-ending 12-game winning streak.

But because only one team from the conference was eligible for the NCAA Tournament, the Hoosiers had no postseason play.

Bob Knight, a reserve for the Buckeyes, later said that IU team might have been the best never to play in the tournament.

Ohio State won on Larry Siegfried's only basket of the game with five seconds to play. The Hoosiers twice lost seven-point leads in the second half and the lead changed hands 14 times. A pair of critical Indiana turnovers in the waning moments opened the door for Siegfried's game winner.

"They can't say they won this one. We gave it to them. We had it won and simply kicked it away," Branch McCracken said in the locker room.

Guard Herbie Lee led IU with 23 points, and sophomore Mel Nowell had 26 for the winners. The first half was such a shootout that IU took a 56-52 lead into the intermission.

Back in Bloomington on Feb. 29, the Hoosiers administered a solid licking to the eventual national champions by handing them their only conference loss.

Lee had been suspended before the rematch, but replacement Gary Long scored 14 points in the first half and the Hoosiers shot 53 percent.

"There wasn't a thing we could do," Ohio State coach Fred Taylor said. "They were just a much better club than we."

It was the last game played in the Seventh Street Fieldhouse.

1962—Indiana 105, Minnesota 104

A rematch of Minnesota's 104-100 victory 19 days earlier, this Jan. 27 game probably marked Jimmy Rayl's greatest day as a Hoosier. The Kokomo junior scored 56 points, still matched only by his 56 the following year against Michigan State.

"It was a tight game. I hit a jump shot to put it into overtime, a pretty long jump shot," Rayl recalled. "That was quite a deal there, I thought."

In Rayl's words: "We were behind by one, 104-103, with seven seconds to go when they hit their last free throw. Jerry Bass threw the ball in to me and when I got across the 10-second line

*Jimmy Rayl was a full-blown Indiana
legend before he even enrolled at IU.
Photo courtesy IU Archives*

I was thinking, 'I can take maybe one or two more dribbles, but I'd better shoot this thing before long.' I may have taken three more dribbles and three more steps, but I know it was a long jump shot. It hit the bottom of the net."

Rayl duplicated his 56 points on Feb. 23, 1963, as the Hoosiers beat visiting Michigan State, 113-94. Jimmy took 48 shots against Michigan State and 39 against Minnesota, the two highest attempt totals in IU history.

McCracken removed Rayl from the Michigan State game with three minutes to play.

"The fans booed him like crazy," Jimmy said.

How many would Rayl have scored had the three-point line been a part of basketball then? It was 25 years later when the three-point play was fully established in college basketball.

Rayl said film of the Minnesota game was lost, leaving no possible answer to that part of the question.

"I know I had 23 field goals against Michigan State and a minimum of 15 or 16 were three-pointers. That would be 71," he said.

Rayl believes a rule change the year after he graduated also contributed to higher scoring.

"They changed it to where the clock stopped for traveling and all kinds of violations. My senior year, if you got called for traveling, or if the ball was knocked into the stands, the clock just kept ticking. The only time a clock stopped was for a jump ball or free throw."

Rayl said a survey the following season indicated the rule change meant an extra five minutes of action.

"Rick Mount got 61," said Rayl, referring to the Big Ten record held by another touted shooter. "If I'd had five minutes I think I could have gotten five extra points."

1996—Indiana 85, Duke 69

The previous night had seen the Hoosiers score an unimpressive 74-73 victory over Evansville in the semifinal round of the Preseason National Invitation Tournament. Junior Andrae Patterson had hit a turnaround jumper at the buzzer to thrust Indiana into the championship game at Madison Square Garden.

Few gave IU much of a chance against Duke in the title game, but a crowd of 17,930 showed up anyway. What the fans saw was the six-foot-eight Patterson scoring 39 points in what was easily the biggest outburst of the soft-spoken Texan's career.

During one 68-second sequence, Patterson made a 10-foot jumper, a 15-footer and then a fancy move that set up an eight-footer. While playing only 34 minutes he made 15 of 24 shots and eight of 10 at the foul line. He also had six rebounds and took home the tournament's Most Valuable Player trophy.

At one point in the second half, Patterson scored 15 straight IU points.

"We had no answer for Patterson," Duke coach Mike Krzyzewski admitted. "He was magnificent. We used bigger guys, smaller guys, two guys and no guys. No guys was about as effective as two guys."

One New York writer predicted that Patterson would cast his lot with the NBA at the end of the season. Instead, he cooled off and averaged just 13.7 points that year.

1991—Ohio State 97, Indiana 95

They were the two best teams in the Big Ten and two of the best in the country. They had the two best players in the conference, the Buckeyes' Jim Jackson and the Hoosiers' Calbert Cheaney. And on a Sunday afternoon they met in the friendly confines of St. John Arena and played what Ohio State coach Randy Ayers said may have been the best game he ever saw.

Damon Bailey was a freshman, and he heard his name chanted hundreds of times that afternoon, every time in derision. Ohio State students sat close to the court and fired every verbal insult known to man at the IU newcomer, whose reputation had been built when he was featured in John Feinstein's book *Season on the Brink* five years earlier.

Bailey never showed an emotion. Not anger. Not reluctance. Instead, he responded with 32 points and, after Cheaney fouled out, took over and scored 12 points in the two overtimes. He also guarded Jackson most of the final 30 minutes and, much to the dismay of the chanting students, didn't make a turnover in 48 minutes.

Ohio State's Treg Lee, who scored the winning basket with three seconds left in the second overtime, said he doubted Bailey's ability entering the game.

"My first impression of Bailey was that I didn't really see why he'd gotten that kind of attention," Lee said.

When Bailey was an eighth grader, Feinstein had quoted Bob Knight as saying, "Damon Bailey is better than any guard we have right now. I don't mean potentially better. I mean better today."

Ohio State entered that game ranked second nationally to Indiana's No. 4. Despite two losses to the Buckeyes that season, the two would tie for the Big Ten title with 15-3 records and continue on to the Sweet Sixteen.

1973—UCLA 70, Indiana 59

With three weeks left in the 1972-73 season, it appeared that Minnesota was a lock for the Big Ten championship. Featuring future baseball star Dave Winfield, the Golden Gophers beat the Hoosiers in Minneapolis, 82-75, to hand the Hoosiers their third loss in the league. But the Gophers stumbled home and Indiana won the Big Ten with an 11-3 record.

The Hoosiers won the rest of their regular-season games and beat Marquette and Kentucky in the first two NCAA Tournament games in Nashville, Tenn. That advanced them to the Final Four for the first time since their title year 20 years earlier.

In their path was UCLA, unbeaten and winner of the last six national championships. The Bruins were led by All-America center Bill Walton, who was outscored by Downing in that meeting 26-14.

The Hoosiers jumped to an early five-point lead, but Downing picked up his third foul as the Bruins were reciprocating with a 29-4 outburst. The lead reached 20 points before the Hoosiers put on a stunning 17-0 run against one of John Wooden's better teams.

Indiana trailed 54-51 when Walton made a move against Downing and was cut off by the Hoosiers' center. Each had four fouls at the time, but the whistle went against Downing.

"Steve turned and it was an obvious Walton foul," said former Hoosier Joby Wright. "They called the foul on Steve. Steve was put out of the game and Walton stayed."

Two nights later, Walton made 21 of 22 shots as UCLA rolled over Memphis State for another national title.

1959—Indiana 122, Ohio State 92

As a sophomore six-foot-one guard, Gary Long averaged nine points a game, so when he broke loose for 29 points against Ohio State in St. John Arena it surprised a lot of people. The next year the Buckeyes captured the NCAA championship.

Indiana's 122 points that night still are as many as any IU team has scored, although the Hoosiers again hit 122 in a 1962 game against Notre Dame.

"I felt like we were in a dream during the whole game," Long said. "Dick Enberg was our announcer, and people were telling us later how he was going wild. The next day in the paper it had a list of the records we had broken. Mostly, I remember it was a fun game and I couldn't believe that it was me doing it. I had pretty much been a benchwarmer up to the game before."

That was against DePaul and marked Long's first collegiate start.

"I got two points in the first half and thought, 'Well, I'm done for,' but then the guy who took my place, Al Schlegelmilch, didn't do very well, either," he recalled. "So I started the second half and got 15 points, and that got me the start at Ohio State."

Indiana had 50 field goals against Ohio State. Other Indiana eruptions included 118 against Iowa in 1990, 117 against Tennessee Tech in 1994 and 116 against the Hawkeyes in 1988.

Chapter 10

The Championship Years

1940

Things looked promising for Indiana as the 1939-40 season approached. Branch McCracken was back for his second season as coach following a rookie year that saw the Hoosiers post a 17-3 record and finish second in the Big Ten.

IU returned 12 lettermen from a team that had been runner-up to Ohio State in 1939. There were Bill and Bob Menke, captain Marvin Huffman, Bob Dro, Jim Gridley, Clarence Ooley, Curly Armstrong, Ralph Dorsey, Tom Motter, Chester Francis and Jack Stevenson.

There was also Herman Schaefer, who had been ineligible the second semester of the '39 season, and Jay McCreary, who was out of school the previous season but who had lettered under Everett Dean in 1937-38. A strong freshman class would produce John and Bill Torphy, Bill Frey and Norman Hasler, among others.

Armstrong, Motter and Schaefer had played together at Fort Wayne Central High School. Huntingburg High also had three represetives in the Menke brothers and Hasler.

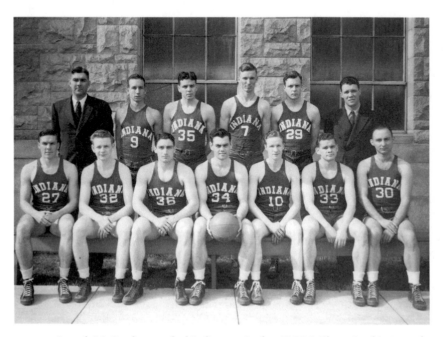

Branch McCracken coached Indiana to its first NCAA Championship in 1940. IU had only one player on the squad taller than 6-feet-4: Andy Zimmer. Photo courtesy IU Archives

Although Piggy Lambert traditionally had strong teams at Purdue, the Boilermakers' squad was younger than usual in 1939-40. Ohio State, which had clinched the championship by beating IU in the season finale the previous year, couldn't be overlooked and Illinois was strong, but the feeling around Bloomington was that Indiana would be the team to beat in the Big Ten.

As it turned out, McCracken's Hurryin' Hoosiers were the team to beat in the nation.

Bill Menke had been the fourth leading scorer in the conference, scoring an impressive 28 points in one game. One of McCracken's concerns was replacing two significant players, All-American Ernie Andres and Bill Johnson.

What would become Indiana's first NCAA championship team featured only one player as tall as six feet four, Andy Zimmer, whose lean frame weighed in at only 175 pounds. But what the Hoosiers lacked in size they replaced with guile and experience, a result of 10 varsity players having played for high school teams that reached the state finals.

McCreary was a standout for the Frankfort Hot Dogs of 1936, a team many considered the state's best during the first half of the 20th century. McCreary would coach a state championship team at Muncie Central before going on to coach Louisiana State University.

Sharpshooting was not paramount at the time, and Bill Menke's 31 percent led the team in 1939. Indiana had five players who shot below 20 percent.

Indiana's soon-to-be championship team had not spent the previous summer lifting weights or otherwise concentrating on the upcoming season. Andy Zimmer had worked on a farm and Chester Francis had raised chickens. Harold Zimmer was a bodyguard. Everett Hoffman clerked in a grocery story and Clarence Ooley was a hotel bellhop. Edward Newby drove a truck. Clifford Wiethoff and Don Huckleberry worked in factories and Thomas Motter worked in a brewery.

But upon returning to campus, the Hoosiers focused on basketball and quickly established themselves as a threat in the Big Ten. Indiana recorded its 16th straight victory on Feb. 12 with a 46-39 triumph over Purdue, which the *Indiana Daily Student* called the "farm-boy school."

That threw the Big Ten race into a deadlock, but Purdue rallied to win the conference at 10-2. Indiana finished alone in second place after blasting third-place Ohio State 52-31 in the regular-season finale, which ran the winning streak at home to 19.

Only a few newspapers at the time referred to Indiana as the Hoosiers. It was much more common to call them the Crimsons, or the Macmen. Another sign of the times involved a rule concerning use of the pressbox: "No women admitted," it read.

Although Indiana was invited to play in the "National Collegiate Tournament," the IU Athletic Board of Control first had to give its permission. Some fans were surprised that Indiana was selected after finishing second in the league, but its two victories over Purdue apparently weighed in its favor.

All three members of the national selection committee, including Butler coach Tony Hinkle, voted to include the Hoosiers.

When all formalities had been handled, the Crimsons defeated Springfield (Mass.) in the opening game at Indianapolis's Butler Fieldhouse, then beat Duquesne 39-30 to reach the national final in Kansas City. In the title game, watched by 10,000 fans in Municipal Auditorium, Indiana pinned a 60-42 loss on Kansas as McCreary scored 12 points.

After falling behind 11-4, IU took a 32-19 halftime lead by making 13 of 39 shots, which an *Indianapolis News* story termed an "amazing" percentage.

The Associated Press story called the five-foot-10 McCreary a gum-chewing blond midget in a forest of physical giants.

The Hoosiers arrived home to ride a fire truck from the north city limits to the men's gym, where a 100-piece band and 2,500 students awaited.

The trip to Kansas City for the title game cost the university a total of $133.45, which included $52.25 for meals and $13 for movies.

Money well spent, most Hoosier fans believed.

1953

Dwight D. Eisenhower had just been elected to the White House, the Korean War was winding down, and optimism flowed in the Seventh Street Fieldhouse as Indiana launched the 1952-53 season with a 39-point victory over Valparaiso, the most lop-sided opener in IU history.

The Big Sheriff, Branch McCracken, finally had his Big Man, six-foot-10 Don Schlundt, and the Hoosiers soon had the supporting cast in guards Bob Leonard and Burke Scott and forwards Dick Farley and Charley Kraak. All were underclassmen, and Schlundt and Scott were only sophomores.

IU had gone 16-6 in 1951-52 but was a modest 9-5 in the conference. Guards Bobby Masters and Sammy Esposito, who would become an infielder with the Chicago White Sox, had moved on. Leonard was set at one guard, but in the preseason Dick Baumgartner, John Wood and Jim DeaKyne were expected to battle for the other backcourt spot. Wood was the younger brother of Marvin Wood, who coached the fabled Milan High team to the 1954 Indiana championship.

Instead, Scott, from Tell City, Indiana, proved to be the perfect match for Leonard.

Indiana's 95-point outburst in the opening game was the second highest in school history, exceeded only by the 96 IU had scored the prior year against Northwestern. The Hurryin' Hoosiers' nickname, a reference to McCracken's speedy and seldom-bashful shooters, caught the imagination of fans around the state and became one of the nation's most colorful monikers.

The Hurryin' Hoosiers became household names through-out Indiana, partly because of the black-and-white telecasts origi-

*The 1953 Hoosiers rejoice around Coach McCracken
after winning their second title in Kansas City.
Photo courtesy IU Archives*

nating from WTTV in Bloomington. Schlundt, a three-time All-American, generally was considered to be the first outstanding big man in the Big Ten. Leonard, later to gain fame as an NBA coach and then as a color commentator at Indiana Pacers games, had the same colorful personality as a young man. He also was one of the headiest players in college basketball and his outside shooting stroke would help make him an All-American.

Farley was tremendously underrated and would become an NBA player. Kraak, the only out-of-state player in the starting lineup, was a solid rebounder who would go on to a high-level military career. Scott was quick and tough and a prototype of what eventually would be termed a point guard.

Some early grumbling surrounded the Hoosiers when they dropped their second and third games of the season, a one-pointer at Notre Dame and a two-pointer at Kansas State. Jack Stephens's basket with two seconds to play won the game for the Irish, and Jack Carby's 40-foot two-handed set shot at the buzzer sealed the victory for Kansas State.

Indiana rebounded from those disappointments to win its next 17 games, a streak that ended on March 7 with a two-point loss at Minnesota.

The Hoosiers would not lose again, concluding a five-game winning streak with a 69-68 win over Kansas for their second NCAA championship.

Schlundt, now the third leading scorer in school history, showed his stuff with a 39-point game at Michigan and followed with 30 at Michigan State. But even a 105-70 victory over Butler—in which Schlundt scored 33—left IU ranked second in the polls to Seton Hall.

The Hurryin' Hoosiers established a Big Ten scoring record on February 23 with a 113-78 blasting of visiting Purdue. They wrapped up their first solo conference championship February 28 with a 91-79 victory over Illinois in which Schlundt scored 33. Illinois center Johnny Kerr, a longtime NBA player, had but 19 against IU's Gentle Giant.

The International News Service ratings at the end of the regular season had Indiana first followed by LaSalle, Seton Hall, North Carolina State, Kansas State, Washington, Oklahoma A&M, Kansas, Illinois and Louisiana State.

The Hurryin' Hoosiers captured two NCAA games in Chicago against DePaul and Notre Dame. Schlundt's 41 points helped Indiana overwhelm one of its early conquerors.

In the Final Four, IU first eliminated LSU 80-67 as Schlundt and the Tigers' All-American, Bob Pettit, each scored 29. Indiana shot 55 percent, outstanding for that era, in winning the semifinal in Kansas City.

The championship game, won by Indiana 69-68 on Leonard's free throw with 27 seconds to play, was one of the NCAA classics. There were 10 ties and neither team led by more than three points in the fourth quarter.

Schlundt had 30 points in a tension-filled game that saw Schlundt and Leonard assessed technicals for remarks to the officials. Kraak also got a technical for elbowing Jayhawk Harold Patterson.

1976

The trademark of the 1976 Hoosiers was defense, especially on the perimeter with guards Bob Wilkerson and Quinn Buckner. Bill Lyon of the *Philadelphia Inquirer* described it as follows:

"It is a demolition defense, and it claws and rakes and pressures until the team with the ball begins to feel like a Christmas shopper, arms loaded with presents, helpless, caught in a revolving door, and there is no way out."

Wilkerson and Buckner may have been the finest set of defensive guards ever assembled, and the front line, led by national Player of the Year Scott May, was no less fearsome. From the season-opening 20-point victory over defending NCAA champion UCLA, the Hoosiers escaped the noose that has encircled every college team since. There were challenges throughout

Quinn Buckner's leadership made the 1973-'76 teams special.
Photo courtesy IU Archive

Indiana's undefeated season but few truly dangerous moments. The most memorable moment came during an overtime win against Michigan in which Kent Benson's buzzer beater forced the extra period.

The Hoosiers won their nine non-conference games by an average of 22.9 points and their 18 Big Ten games by an average of 15.7 points. May, a defensive force as well as a 23.5 scorer as a senior, had a 41-point night against Wisconsin. Benson, the only underclassman starting, was a dominant scorer and All-American. Coach Bob Knight generally recognized Buckner as his best leader ever.

The NCAA Tournament started in South Bend with a 20-point win over St. John's and continued in Baton Rouge, where Alabama and Marquette were sidelined. In the Final Four in Philadelphia the Hoosiers beat UCLA for the second time, 65-51, and Michigan for the third, 86-68. Unlike the previous year when May broke his arm, these Hoosiers escaped injury in the tournament until three minutes into the title game when Wilkerson sustained a concussion. But after trailing 35-29 at halftime, IU erupted for 57 points in the second half to hand Michigan the loss. The average margin of victory in five tournament games was 13. Yet many still claim that the 1975 team was even better. That team was unbeaten until an injury to May contributed to a two-point loss to Kentucky in the NCAA.

With each passing year Indiana's unbeaten season looms larger. Only seven teams have gone undefeated and all did so after 1956. Each of IU's five starters, which also included Tom Abernethy, played in the NBA for at least five years.

1981

A chance meeting in late December at the Kansas City Airport saw Knight and North Carolina coach Dean Smith commiserate about each other's problems. The Hoosiers were returning home from the Rainbow Classic in Honolulu, where they had lost two out of three games, giving them a 7-5 record.

Kent Benson, a heralded center from New Castle, Ind.,
was the only underclass starter on the unbeaten 1976 team.
Photo courtesy IU Archives

"Going out to Hawaii was miserable, and when we got back we had three-a-days for the next week," former Hoosier Steve Risley said years later. "There were times when we felt like we were subhuman. It wasn't torture or anything like that; it was just Knight's way of working us out of it."

When Knight and Smith crossed paths, the Tar Heels were also struggling.

"He had just been beaten by Minnesota at a tournament in Los Angeles by 16 points. They had just killed them," Knight recalled in 1991. "We were standing there talking about what we were trying to do and how we were trying to play, and neither one of us was doing real well at that point."

Three months later Indiana would beat the Tar Heels 63-50 for the NCAA championship.

While the Hoosiers finished the season with nine losses, few teams have been stronger in their run to the championship. After winning its last five regular-season games, IU opened NCAA play by blistering Maryland 99-64 in Dayton, Ohio, in what may have been as close to a perfect game as an IU team has ever played.

The Hoosiers made 41 of 63 shots in disposing of Lefty Driesell's touted Terrapins. Isiah Thomas made nine of 11 shots in the game. Ray Tolbert was 10 of 13 and Landon Turner hit nine of 13. Thomas had 14 assists and 19 points. Tolbert scored 26 points and had five dunks.

Driesell could only say, "I ain't never got beat that bad."

The Hoosiers' Jim Thomas said the preparation put into facing Maryland was the best he has seen for a college game.

"We came in as a bit of an underdog, having lost so many games at that point, and Maryland had a slew of players who would play in the NBA," Thomas said.

"We had a lot to prove, but we felt if we could come back to Bloomington with the win we had an excellent chance to go to the Final Four. When we went into that game we were in the mindset of knowing what we had to do."

Ted Kitchel recalled a Maryland assistant coach pointing out the Indiana players to Driesell during pregame warmups.

*Isiah Thomas was the hub of Indiana's 1981
champions, then departed after the season for the NBA.
Photo courtesy IU Archives*

"I don't think that, other than Isiah Thomas, he knew who the hell any of us were," Kitchel said.

The Hoosiers saw a window of opportunity because St. Joseph's had upset top-seeded DePaul. After defeating Alabama-Birmingham on its own court, Indiana beat Pennsylvania 78-46 to advance to the Final Four.

"We had some moments where we would rival what the '76 team did, but I think the '76 team was able to maintain a level of excellence, not only during the regular season but in the tournament. But we played some excellent ball in 1981," Jim Thomas recalled.

Returning to Philadelphia, the site of its 1976 championship, IU drilled LSU by 18 and North Carolina by 13. Trailing by one at halftime, Indiana quickly put away the Tar Heels in the second half as Isiah Thomas scored 19 of his 23 points after half-time.

1987

Knight's '87 Hoosiers exceeded even his expectations.

"I said all along that I didn't think we were a team that was a national champion," Knight said. "We will not go down in history as one of the dominant NCAA champs."

Two things were significant in Indiana capturing its fifth NCAA championship in 1987. One, the three-point field goal had just become a fixture in college basketball. Two, Bob Knight adjusted the philosophy that had made him reluctant to recruit junior college players.

Knight already had the nucleus of a national contender in senior guard Steve Alford, who would utilize the three-point shot to the full extent, and forwards Daryl Thomas and Rick Calloway. When he added two junior college transfers, athletic guard Keith Smart and center Dean Garrett, Indiana again was a program to fear.

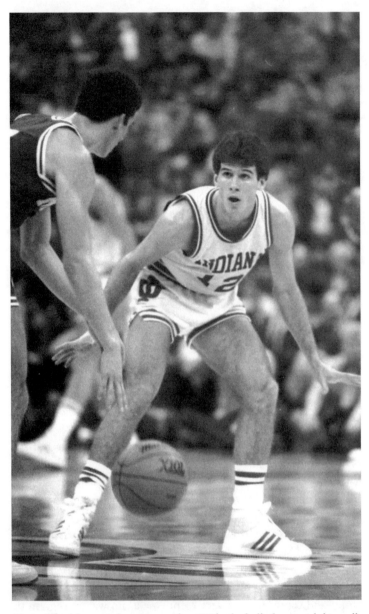

Steve Alford became the epitome of an IU basketball player with his well-groomed look, but the prettiest part about him was his jump shot.
Photo courtesy IU Archives

Knight's decision to recruit Smart and Garrett came after another highly sought junior college player, Andre Harris, had experienced academic problems.

"After what happened to Andre we wanted to prove something, that junior college players aren't all academic failures or failures in any aspect," Garrett said.

Smart, who had a 46-inch vertical leap, was only five-foot-three as a high school junior and missed most of his senior season with a broken arm. Thus, he enrolled at Garden City Junior College in Kansas before moving on to Indiana.

Only one year earlier author John Feinstein had written the national bestseller, *Season on the Brink*, which detailed the turmoil of a 21-8 season that ended with a stunning loss to Cleveland State in the opening game of the NCAA Tournament.

In '87 the Hoosiers won 14 of their first 15 games, the exception a 79-75 defeat at Vanderbilt. The second loss was at top-ranked Iowa, 101-88, but that was followed by nine more victories. One of those was a triple-overtime struggle at Wisconsin, giving the Hoosiers a 23-2 record.

Successive road losses to Purdue and Illinois popped the balloon, but IU would win its next seven, including the 74-73 title game against Syracuse.

Smart's 15-foot jumper with four seconds left saw him elevate over defender Howard Triche, who was four inches taller, to seal the national championship. The winning basket wasn't a set play and it came after an alert Thomas, who was covered by a taller Derrick Coleman, flipped the basketball back to the equally alert Smart. Their heroics were necessary because Syracuse was focusing on stopping Alford, who was well covered.

"I shot-faked and shot-faked, but Coleman didn't move," Thomas said. "I didn't want to take a bad shot, so I kicked it back out to Keith."

"I've made that shot a thousand times before on the playground. That's a pickup game shot," Smart said.

Alford's basket at the end of the first half was almost as memorable, and as important, as Smart's game-ending basket. Starting at the top of the lane Alford ran around a pick by Todd Meier and shot down the right side of the lane as Smart passed to Joe Hillman just inside the three-point line. Alford cut along the baseline to the right corner and circled around Hillman, who screened center Rony Seikaly as Alford drained the three-point shot for a one-point IU lead.

Hardly pausing, the Indiana senior headed off the corner of the court toward the locker room.

AP/WWP

SPECIAL THANKS TO THE FOLLOWING
FOR THEIR SUPPORT OF
THIS BOOK.

Huse Incorporated

www.huseinc.com • (812) 332-4838